W9-BAI-214

Guided Reading

A Practical Approach for Teachers

Guided Reading

A Practical Approach for Teachers

The Wright Group®

19201 120th Avenue NE • Bothell, WA 98011

Guided Reading: A Practical Approach for Teachers

© 1995 Wright Group Publishing, Inc.

This guide includes material from the *SUNSHINE*™ *Level 1 Teacher Guide* and the *SUNSHINE*™ *Levels 2–5 Teacher Guide.*

Chart 8, "Error and Accuracy Rates," is based on an accuracy rate table in *The Early Detection of Reading Difficulties* by Marie Clay, published in the United States by Heinemann (3d ed., 1985). Used with permission of Octopus Publishing Group Ltd., New Zealand.

Photography: David Perry and Steve Young

All rights reserved. No part of this book may be reproduced or transmitted in any form without written authorization from The Wright Group permissions department, with the exception of the reproducibles on pages 75–81. Unlimited reproduction rights for these reproducibles are granted to the individual classroom teacher purchasing this teacher guide.

The Wright Group
19201 120th Avenue NE
Bothell, WA 98011

Printed in the United States of America

10 9 8 7 6 5

ISBN: 0-7802-3007-8

Contents

Chapter 1
Introduction to Guided Reading

What Is Guided Reading?

Guided Reading is one process used in teaching children to read. Guided Reading is a group approach, involving the teacher with a small group of children of similar reading ability. The teacher selects an appropriate book for the group, a book that is at the children's instructional reading level and that will introduce or reinforce appropriate reading challenges for that particular group of children.

The teacher spends the first part of a Guided Reading session discussing the concepts of the book and scaffolding information, thereby laying a foundation for reading success. At the emergent levels, the teacher guides the children in exploring the language structure and vocabulary of the story prior to the first reading. In this way, the children already understand the sentence structure of the book and recognize most of the key words, so the groundwork for a successful reading experience is in place before the children begin to read. The teacher also discusses reading strategies with the children during Guided Reading, helping the children to identify and utilize many ways to solve print problems.

Children may read the entire story two or more times during a Guided Reading session. At the earliest levels of Guided Reading, the children read aloud together, with each child reading at his or her own pace. At more advanced levels, the children read silently and then together discuss the story and their use of reading strategies. The Guided Reading process works be-

cause it provides several structured opportunities for successful reading and because children are not singled out to read individually.

During Guided Reading, the teacher has an opportunity to evaluate each child's reading in action. Just as the Guided Reading experience is structured to promote successful reading by children, it is also structured to encourage successful evaluation of children's use of print concepts and reading strategies. Through the use of appropriate strategy prompts, the teacher can focus a child on a specific concept of print, on a particular cue system, or on a particular reading strategy. Because the children are in a group situation, they can all be helped with a particular challenge, or one child can be helped with a specific problem in a nonthreatening way.

As the children gain experience and competency in their reading, they will advance toward reading independence as the teacher gradually withdraws his or her support in the Guided Reading process. Eventually the children will progress into silent Guided Reading, reading the book silently by themselves and then coming together to discuss the story in beginning literature circles.

Children at each developmental level of reading need an appropriate format for Guided Reading sessions. The formats change as reading ability progresses. Gradually the amount of support by the teacher and by the group is reduced as children become more competent. This teacher guide includes suggested formats for Guided Reading at each level of reading along with strategy prompts and models of actual Guided Reading lessons.

You may adapt and rearrange these formats and models to fit the needs of your students. (For example, you may choose to combine two steps of a format to better suit the needs of your Guided Reading groups or your classroom time schedule.) The formats and models provided in this teacher guide are meant to serve as possible examples and not as prescriptions.

Guided Reading sessions also include mini language lessons that introduce or reinforce concepts of print or concepts of literature. Discussion as part of the Guided Reading session may include retellings or responses to the story. Discussion is also a good way to connect a story to the children's own experiences. Follow-up activities can extend a Guided Reading session into content areas or different modes of creative expression. Follow-up activities to Guided Reading are most appropriate when they solidify the meaning of a story.

At first, Guided Reading can seem complex and difficult, just as reading does to children at the emergent level. But incorporating Guided Reading into your classroom routine is a process of growth. As you become more familiar with the Guided Reading approach, it will become an integral part of your reading program.

This manual was designed to provide you with the information and examples you need to begin doing effective Guided Reading sessions in your classroom. Specific attention has been paid to helping you understand the changes in Guided Reading that need to occur as children develop their skills and gradually take over the process to become independent readers.

The Balanced Reading Program

Children benefit in different ways from different kinds of reading experiences. Therefore, classrooms that use a combination of approaches in a flexible format are those most likely to give all children the chance to read successfully.

The Balanced Reading Program incorporates seven basic processes that involve both independent and interactive reading and writing experiences:

1. Reading Aloud to Children
2. Shared Reading
3. Guided Reading
4. Paired Reading
5. Independent Reading
6. Language Exploration
7. Writing and Reading: The Balanced Writing Program

Reading *to* children, *with* children, and *by* children are key features of the Balanced Reading Program—and of the entire day—in a whole-language classroom. These processes are not meant to be confined to a stipulated reading/writing time. Rather, they are part and parcel of all classroom activities. (You may find it helpful to refer to chart 1, "Integration of Reading and Writing Processes," on page 4 as you read the following pages.)

Reading Aloud to Children
Reading aloud to children from the best children's literature available should be a daily part of the reading program. Selections chosen to read aloud should include all genres of fiction and nonfiction. Teachers who read aloud every day demonstrate that reading is enjoyable and important. Reading to children also helps familiarize them with the language of books and its patterns, as well as a variety of basic reading conventions. In addition, reading aloud allows children to hear language that may be above their present independent reading level but perfectly suitable for their "listening" level.

Shared Reading
Shared Reading is an interactive reading experience enjoyed by the whole class. Children join

Paired Reading

Paired reading gives children the opportunity to work together in pairs and help each other learn how to read. These pairs can be of many types: children can be at the same ability level or at different levels, and they can be the same age or different ages. Buddy reading, partner reading, and shared practice are other names for paired reading.

Independent Reading

Independent reading is both part of and the goal of learning to read. Children learn to read by reading, so they need time to read appropriate materials by themselves. "Appropriate" in this context refers to books or other reading materials that the children are able to read with confidence. This confidence is vital in attaining independence. Independent reading material may come from your classroom library, the school library, Guided Reading book boxes (either individual book boxes or Guided Reading group book boxes), the Big Book center, the poetry/music corner, and so on.

Language Exploration

Language exploration (literacy activities) involves children in further development of any experience through discussion, reading, writing, art, music, drama, and a wide array of other activities. Language exploration engages children in all of the communication skills: speaking, reading, writing, listening, observing, illustrating, experiencing, and doing.

Writing and Reading: The Balanced Writing Program

Writing is an integral part of a language program and is especially important in aiding beginning readers to develop their written skills as they did oral skills—through approximations. Children who write by themselves learn a great deal that will help them with reading and vice versa. Writing also reinforces the message that the purpose of written language is communication. For more information on the writing process, consult the *SUNSHINE™ Level 1 Teacher Guide* and the *SUNSHINE™ Levels 2–5 Teacher Guide* (both available from The Wright Group).

in on key words and phrases that they know as the teacher reads a story aloud. The children read more and more of the text in subsequent rereadings until they are able to read the story independently.

Guided Reading

Guided Reading, which is the focus of this book, is an approach that enables a teacher and a small group of children to think about, talk about, and read a book together for a specific purpose. The teacher guides the group in reading through a story that the children will later read independently. Monitoring and evaluating progress are done during this reading. (The following chapters describe Guided Reading in detail. They include formats for different reading levels and models of actual Guided Reading sessions.)

Before You Begin a Guided Reading Program

Developing a Literate Environment

Before you begin a Guided Reading program in your classroom, you will want to lay a strong foundation in daily reading and writing activities. Children should be regularly engaging in the following reading and writing activities as part of the classroom day:

- Shared Reading, singing, reciting poetry, reading, and being read to

- Talking about stories and discussing them openly

- Responding to stories through reproductions, retellings, innovations, dramatic reenactments, and other artistic creations

- Reading stories independently

- Writing daily in a wide variety of forms, such as stories, journals, diaries, letters, and logs

- Working on Daily News activities and other written language experiences

As a result of all these reading and writing experiences, the literate classroom is filled with children's responses and creations.

Chart 1

Integration of Reading and Writing Processes

Schedule		Reading Process	Writing Process
9:00	Greeting Daily News	Language Exploration	Model Writing Language Exploration
9:30	Writing Workshop	Shared Reading Independent Reading	Model Writing Journal Writing
10:15	Poetry		Process Writing Guided Writing
10:45	Literature/Literacy	Shared Reading Guided Reading Independent Reading	Content Writing Structure Writing Nonfiction Writing
11:45	Songs, Read-aloud Story	Shared Reading Reading Aloud	
12:00	**Lunch**		
1:00	Math/Science Environments	Chart Reading Pattern Reading	Recording Observations Charting Sorting/Classifying
1:45	Practice Journals	Shared Reading Independent Reading	Structure Writing
2:00	Thematic Activities	Content Reading Language Exploration	Content Writing Language Exploration
2:45	Summary Sharing	Language Exploration	Language Exploration
3:00	**Home**		

Developing Independent Learners

Before you begin to add Guided Reading groups to your program, you must be confident in the children's ability to function responsibly and independently in your classroom.

- Establish strong learning routines that revolve around a variety of reading-related activities.

- Consider setting up interactive or independent reading and learning centers.

Finding an Appropriate Space

Before you begin Guided Reading groups, you will need to evaluate your classroom arrangement.

1. Set aside a specific area for meeting with your Guided Reading groups. Options for this include:

   - Teacher and children all sitting at a table

   - Children sitting on the floor in a semicircle with the teacher sitting on a chair

   - Teacher and children all sitting on the floor in either a semicircle or circle

2. Have the quietest reading centers or activities closest to the Guided Reading area and the noisier or more interactive activities farther away.

3. Position yourself to best observe the entire classroom.

4. Have your Guided Reading books and materials convenient for easy access.

Selecting Books for Guided Reading

Selecting books for use with Guided Reading groups is an important part of your planning. Every book you select for use with a Guided Reading group must be at the appropriate instructional reading level for that group. This step is especially critical at the emergent levels. Books for Guided Reading at the emergent levels must have rhyme, rhythm, and repetition, or children cannot use all three reading cue systems (discussed below). At the early fluency level, you have more flexibility in your choice of books for Guided Reading groups.

Books selected for Guided Reading should be challenging, but not too difficult. The children should be able to read approximately 90 to 95 percent of the words in the story. Stories containing a high percentage of known words allow children to use meaning as the dominant cue system, which helps them to make more accurate predictions and to apply more than one reading strategy to unknown words. Yet stories should provide enough of a challenge so that they require students to actually do some reading work. It is this reading work that enables students to develop and refine their reading strategies.

Specific characteristics of books at each developmental level are included later in this chapter in the section on the developmental levels of reading. Of course, an additional factor is the available number of copies of a selected book, as you need one copy of the book for each child in a Guided Reading group.

The Three Reading Cue Systems and the Reading Process

Because reading is such a complex undertaking, no single strategy works best to teach reading. Rather, many useful strategies should be employed. Developmentally, children first connect with books through the rich experiences and emotions stories bring to their lives. A child who is read to at home is often found "rereading" a beloved story by using the pictures and the memory of the story line for retelling (semantics). Later, the child will be able to say more of the text using the memory of phrases (syntactics or syntax). The more repetitive the story text, the easier it is for the child to make connections between what is remembered, what is heard, and what is written. Gradually, the child makes a clearer match between what he or she says and what is written. The child may substitute words like *mom* for *mother* or *bunny* for *rabbit*, but the meaning remains the same.

Children will read and reread favorite stories until they master them. They begin to look very carefully at words. They may notice beginning or ending letters or check a word with one on a previous page to see if they are the same (graphophonics). Once they are able to read every word perfectly, they then look for another book to master.

We need to focus readers' attention on using all three reading cue systems—the semantic, the syntactic, and the graphophonic—in an integrated way. Studies have shown that the best readers use all three reading cue systems when

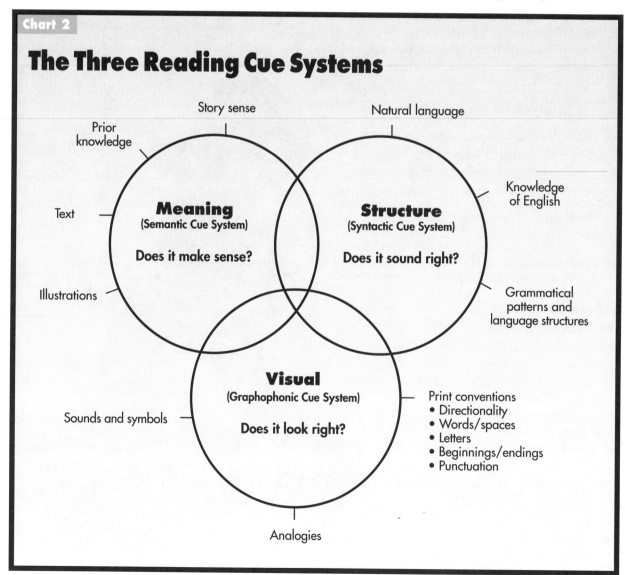

Chart 2

The Three Reading Cue Systems

Story sense

Prior knowledge

Natural language

Meaning
(Semantic Cue System)

Does it make sense?

Structure
(Syntactic Cue System)

Does it sound right?

Knowledge of English

Text

Illustrations

Grammatical patterns and language structures

Visual
(Graphophonic Cue System)

Does it look right?

Sounds and symbols

Print conventions
• Directionality
• Words/spaces
• Letters
• Beginnings/endings
• Punctuation

Analogies

they read. The poorest readers use only one system, the graphophonic. (For more on these concepts, see the works of Ken Goodman and Yetta Goodman and Marie Clay.)

When children use semantic cues, they use their prior knowledge and understanding of the meaning of the story line to help them read. Children want what they read to make sense.

Syntactic cues involve children in the use of a book's grammatical patterns and language structures in addition to their current knowledge of the English language. Children who are second-language learners, children who have strong dialects, or children with minimal literary experiences may have problems with the structure of the written text.

Graphophonic cues deal with the relationship between sounds and symbols and the child's understanding of visual and spatial concepts. In general, children need to understand the concepts of word/space and word/letter before they can begin using and identifying sounds/symbols in their reading.

When we read for information or pleasure, rather than as an exercise or a drill, we always read words within the context of other words. To access the semantic and syntactic cue systems, children must read words that are in a meaningful context. By teaching children how to read words only in isolation (graphophonics), providing them with only one cue system, we fail to show them the variety of strategies that exist in real reading situations. By teaching children how to use all of the cue systems in their reading from the beginning, we provide them with the variety of reading strategies they need to become successful readers.

Children can be viewed as being at one of four levels in their reading development: early emergent, upper emergent, early fluency, or fluency. A Guided Reading session will vary in the method of presentation, in the difficulty of books selected, and in the focus skills at each developmental level. The differences are discussed below.

Early Emergent Level

READER PROFILE

Early emergent readers are just learning that illustrations and books tell a story. Because the beginning books for this level are designed to be instant readers, children do not need to learn letters or vocabulary words prior to reading. The repetition of a single phrase, the use of natural language, and the clear matching of each illustration to the corresponding text make it possible for any child to read on the first day of school. At the early emergent level, children often memorize the text as part of the developmental process. Children at this level are most often found in K–1 classrooms. However, the teaching procedures can apply to any grade and to ESL students.

FOCUS SKILLS

Early emergent is an appropriate level for children who need practice and guidance in these concepts or skills:

- Front and back of a book
- Title and title page
- Top and bottom of a page
- Where to begin on a page
- Left-to-right progression and return sweep (directionality)
- Print contains meaning
- Word/space
- First and last word
- One-to-one correspondence (word match)
- Recognizing some letters
- Basic punctuation (period, question mark)
- Learning some high-frequency words (a minimum of ten)

BOOK CHARACTERISTICS

Books appropriate for early emergent readers have

- Rhyme, rhythm, repetition, and natural language

- Illustrations that match the text

- Left-to-right flow of illustrations to reinforce left-to-right reading orientation

- A cover and title page that are integral parts of the whole book

- Repetitive sequences that introduce simple one-word changes at the end of each sequence

- A careful introduction of small changes, such as a one-word change on each page, combined with visual clues and word patterns to help children use the semantic cue system to predict and confirm text

- Simple story beginnings, middles, and endings

- A combination of readily available clues to help children begin using more than one reading strategy; examples are picture clues, visual clues, clues from text, and meaning clues

- Surprise endings or twists on the story

Upper Emergent Level

READER PROFILE

Upper emergent readers grasp many of the basic concepts of print and are ready for more complex stories. These students are developing independence by beginning to integrate strategies and to gain meaning from print. Children at the upper emergent level are most often found in grades K–1. However, the teaching procedures may apply to any grade and to ESL students.

FOCUS SKILLS

The upper emergent level is appropriate for children who need practice or guidance in these skills:

- Building their prior knowledge or solidifying their knowledge of concepts of word/space, first/last word, one-to-one word match, and words/letters

- Identifying high-frequency words (a minimum of twenty)

- Identifying most or all letters

- Recognizing basic punctuation marks

- Indentifying initial consonants

- Beginning to use reading strategies and cue systems

BOOK CHARACTERISTICS

Books appropriate for upper emergent readers have

- Sentences replacing captions or longer sentences replacing shorter ones

- Dialogue mixed with prose and a variety of dialogue formats

- Text that no longer corresponds as directly to the illustrations

- Illustrations that increasingly serve as sources for confirmation rather than prediction

- Two or more words introduced in a writing structure rather than one

- Illustrations as only a small part of the story content

- Increased vocabulary and text that may pose questions; children predict answers by referring to both text and illustrations

Early Fluency Level

READER PROFILE

Early fluency readers are beginning to achieve independence by integrating meaning, structures, and varied text. Books at this level still continue to provide some repetitive and relevant story situations and to build on vocabulary already introduced. Early fluency readers are still developing an understanding of plots, character, and simple literary elements. Children at the early fluency level are most often found in first or second grade. However, the teaching procedures may apply to any grade and to ESL students.

FOCUS SKILLS

Basic reading development skills that students acquire at the early fluency level include

- Taking risks without fear of making errors
- Using picture clues as a means of cross-checking
- Reading on to gain meaning
- Using first/last consonants
- Increasing sight vocabulary (a minimum of forty words)
- Retelling stories
- Identifying punctuation marks
- Solidifying their knowledge of lowercase/capital letters

- Rereading for meaning
- Self-correcting
- Integrating strategies by using one strategy to cross-check another
- Inferring more from the text to comprehend fully the author's intent

BOOK CHARACTERISTICS

Books appropriate for early fluency readers have

- More complex story lines
- More fully developed characters and plots, and interactions between the two
- New challenges in language usage, such as similes and metaphors
- Paragraphs instead of simple sentences
- Illustrations with many details that not only support the story meaning but also create story atmosphere
- Story lines involving different cultures, times, and settings

Fluency Level

READER PROFILE

Fluency level readers are reading fluently, using reading strategies effectively and becoming involved in stories at deeper levels of understanding. Students are working cooperatively as part of literature circles on a variety of genres, stories, and topics. Children at the fluency level are most often found in second grade and on.

FOCUS SKILLS

The basic reading development skills that children should master at the fluency level are

- Increased fluency
- The ability to read text independently
- The successful use and integration of reading strategies
- An understanding of basic literary elements

BOOK CHARACTERISTICS

Books for fluency level readers are any literature selections that are at the appropriate reading and emotional levels of the readers.

Guided Reading Formats

As children progress through the developmental levels of reading, the Guided Reading formats change to meet the developing needs of the learners. Each format is discussed in detail in chapters 2–4. These progressive levels are shown in chart 3, "Developmental Levels in Guided Reading."

Early Emergent Level

In Guided Reading at the early emergent level, the focus is on acquiring the beginning reading skills such as concepts of print and on using beginning reading strategies such as looking at illustrations. The children in a Guided Reading group at this level are generally engaged in simultaneous oral reading with a great deal of teacher guidance and support.

Upper Emergent Level

In Guided Reading at the upper emergent level, two formats help to provide a transition from simultaneous oral reading to silent Guided Reading:

Format 1 focuses on strategy development. Initially, you may hide the text with your hand when you introduce a new book for Guided Reading. Then students simultaneously read aloud the new selection using their knowledge of reading strategies. In this format, you prompt, discuss, and reinforce the children's use of strategies. Once students have grasped the concept of one-to-one correspondence and have a solid foundation of sight words, the Guided Reading process shifts to silent Guided Reading and increased independence with the following format.

Format 2 at the upper emergent level continues to focus on strategy development, but students are now guided to silently locate and confirm story text. At this level, you begin to withdraw support as students become more independent in their use of strategies.

Early Fluency Level

The early fluency level also has two suggested formats for helping students to master their strategies and to become more independent readers prior to moving into literature circles at the fluency level. Format 1 at the early fluency level focuses on mastery of reading strategies as students continue to predict and to confirm text and begin reading longer sections silently.

Format 2 continues to focus on the mastery of reading strategies as students move into a more in-depth study of literary elements in preparation for literature circles. By this time, students need only minimal support and guidance and are taking on much of the responsibility for their own learning and literature involvement.

Key Elements of Guided Reading

Guided Reading lessons at all three levels—early emergent, upper emergent, and early fluency—have several key elements in common. It is important to understand these elements before proceeding with the actual Guided Reading process.

Discussion and Cognitive Webs

As you introduce and initially discuss the story, you need to find out what the children know and what they still need to know about the story topic. From this information, you can develop cognitive webs, which will help facilitate the students' personal connection to the story and build scaffolds for continued learning. These webs may be developed through group discussions, other reading materials, charts or mapping activities, manipulatives, or physical activities.

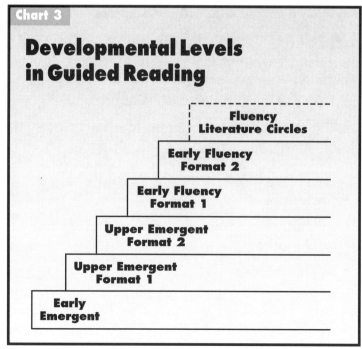

Chart 3

Developmental Levels in Guided Reading

Fluency
Literature Circles

Early Fluency
Format 2

Early Fluency
Format 1

Upper Emergent
Format 2

Upper Emergent
Format 1

Early
Emergent

Follow-up discussions may also help solidify meaning for the students. Additional cognitive webs and other literary devices may be used or discussed at this time.

Picture Walk

Open-ended questions encourage students to "read through" the pictures to gain a sense of the story. The picture walk helps students to focus on illustrations instead of the text and gives them a point of reference when reading the story. Picture walks may vary in length. Depending on the children's experiences and abilities, you may have them look at the first two or three pages of the story or walk them through the whole story.

Implanting Language

During the initial discussion or picture walk, you can orally "plant" unusual vocabulary words or sentence structures that may be unfamiliar. This implanting of language serves as a further resource for children to draw upon when they first encounter new text.

For example, in a book about the zoo, the first page of text might be, "Look at the monkeys." Ask the children to describe what they see in the illustration on that page (monkeys). Then respond, "So if you were at the zoo, you might say, 'Look at the _____.'" The children should then supply the word *monkeys*. This process gives the children the structure found throughout the book as well as the first descriptive noun, thereby encouraging successful reading of the first page.

Strategy Questions

Readers use *cues* to gain information from the text. Good readers use three major cue systems (meaning/semantics, structure/syntax, and visual/graphophonics) as they read. *Strategies* are how the reader makes use of the cues. Children can be encouraged and guided to use specific strategies as they read. The teacher can ask focused questions that direct students to use a specific strategy.

From *meaning* cues, readers associate language with experience and gain an understanding of what is happening in the story.

- To focus a child on meaning cues, you might say

"Did that make sense?"

"Look at the pictures."

"What happened in the story when _____?"

"What do you think it might be?"

From *structure* cues, readers understand and use their knowledge of language patterns and grammatical structures.

- To focus a child on structure cues, you might say

"Did that sound right?"

"Can you reread that?"

"Can you say it that way?"

"What is another word that might fit here?"

From *visual* cues, readers identify letter-sound relationships through their visual knowledge or the associated sounds.

- To focus a child on visual cues, you might say

"Does that look right?"

"What letter/sound does it start/end with?"

"What would you expect to see at the beginning/in the middle/at the end?"

"Do you know another word that might start/end with those letters?"

"Can you get your mouth ready to say that word/sound?"

Self-correcting strategies are evident when readers correct a miscue in their reading. This self-correction is an important step toward independence in reading. When children self-correct, they have noticed that something is wrong, they have taken a closer look at the text, or they have applied another strategy to try to correct the miscue.

- To focus a child on self-correcting, you might say

"There is a difficult [or "tricky"] part here. Can you find it?"

"Are you right? Could that be _____?"

"Take a closer look at _____."

"How did you know that this word was _____?"

Readers are using *cross-checking* strategies when they check one strategy against another while reading. Once students are able to cross-check using more than one strategy, they have gained even greater independence in reading.

- To focus a child on cross-checking, you might say

  "How did you know that was _____? Is there another way to tell?"

  "It could be _____, but look at _____."

Readers have developed *self-monitoring* strategies when they check their own reading behaviors. Self-monitoring is the ultimate goal of Guided Reading.

- To focus a child on self-monitoring, you might say

  "Try that again."

  "What did you notice?"

  "Were you right?"

  "How did you know?"

  "Why did you stop?"

Using Multiple Cue Systems

Every reader should become competent in using *all three* cue systems automatically. Three examples of error correction using multiple cue systems are discussed below. In these examples, *C* stands for *child* and *T* stands for *teacher*.

EXAMPLE 1

The child in this example reads *puppy* for *dog*. This child uses meaning and structure cues but does not attend to visual cues. Therefore, the teacher guides the child to use visual cues.

Text: *I see the dog.*

C: I see the puppy.

T: *(Has student point to the word* dog.*)* You are right. *Puppy* does make sense in this sentence and it sounds right, but could this word be *puppy?* What letter would *puppy* begin with?

C: *P.*

T: Can you find the letter *p* in this word?

C: No.

T: What letter does this word begin with?

C: *D.*

T: What word could you use here instead of *puppy* that begins with the letter *d?*

C: *Dog.*

T: Could this word be *dog?* Does *dog* look right here? Try using *dog* in this sentence to see if it works.

C: *(Rereads correctly.)*

T: Good job of looking at the word *dog.*

EXAMPLE 2

The child in this example uses visual and structure cues but does not use meaning. In this instance, the teacher focuses on meaning.

Text: *I see the dog.*

C: I see the dish.

T: *(Has student point to the word* dog.*)* You are right that this word starts like *dish*, but does *dish* make sense in this sentence? Look at the picture and see what might make sense in this story.

C: There is a dog in the picture.

T: Would *dog* make sense in this story? Read the sentence again and see if *dog* makes sense.

C: *(Rereads correctly.)*

T: Does *dog* make sense in the story now? Good job of using meaning in your reading.

EXAMPLE 3

The child in the following example uses visual cues but does not attend to structure or meaning.

Text: *I see the dog.*

C: I seven the dog.

T: *(Has student point to the word* see.*)* You are right that *seven* and this word begin the same, but read the sentence again and see if it sounds right or makes sense.

C: *(Rereads.)*

T: What other word begins like *seven* but would sound right and make sense here?

C: *(Rereads and corrects.)*

T: You're right. *See* makes the sentence sound right, and now it makes sense, doesn't it?

Evaluation

Students are constantly monitored and evaluated while participating in Guided Reading. You need to observe

- What strategies the child is using successfully

- What strategies need to be modeled

- What strategies are not present

- What letters and sound skills the child knows

Evaluation can occur any time you observe children read throughout the day. As you monitor the children, you need to bring to a conscious level those skills and strategies that the children use by calling their attention to what they did right or by guiding a child to use a particular strategy.

See Chapter 6 for more specific information about evaluation of reading.

Mini Language Lessons

You can focus on a specific skill, strategy, or reading concept at any point in the Guided Reading process. You can decide when a mini language lesson is applicable based on the needs of one or more of the students. Throughout a single Guided Reading session, you may choose to conduct from one to several minilessons at various points. These lessons may last anywhere from a few seconds during a session to three to five minutes following the reading.

Related Activities

You can use a variety of related literacy-oriented activities to extend and enrich the children's involvement with the story. However, these activities should not be done with every story—once or twice a week is enough. The activity booklets accompanying the Guided Reading kits suggest activities relating to the books provided in each kit.

Grouping for Guided Reading

An ideal Guided Reading group includes from two to five children with each child using his or her own copy of the book. The rest of the class can be occupied with related reading activities or independent reading.

Children at the emergent level are grouped homogeneously for Guided Reading so that you can focus on concepts of print and reading strategies in detail. Children at the early fluency level can be grouped more heterogeneously as you deal with concepts of literature and move into beginning literature circles.

Summary

Every aspect of a Guided Reading session is focused on providing the right amount of support and guidance for the children to become independent readers. The process changes at each level to shift more and more of the responsibility to the children.

Children beginning Guided Reading at the early emergent level practice reading aloud together with a great deal of teacher support. As they progress from one level or format to the next, they gain in their independence as readers. Once children reach the early fluency level, they are reading silently with only minimal teacher support. Students become more involved in beginning literature circles at the early fluency level as they become more self-sufficient readers.

Independence is also stressed as children are guided to use all three cue systems independently and effectively as early as possible. Effective reading behaviors are constantly modeled and reinforced. As children progress, they are guided to use more effective strategies and are encouraged to cross-check their reading using two or more cue systems. Students are encouraged to ask themselves three questions when they encounter a "tricky" or unknown word: Does it make sense? Does it sound right? Does it look right? Once they have mastered these strategies based on the three cue systems, they are well on their way to becoming independent, fluent readers. They have begun to develop a self-monitoring process that will assist them in reading for any purpose.

Chapter 2

Early Emergent Level

This chapter gives a suggested format for Guided Reading at the early emergent level. The outline of the basic Guided Reading format is followed by a more detailed description of each step of the format. After the format is explained, two Guided Reading models follow. These include transcripts of actual classroom Guided Reading sessions and explanations of or comments on the teacher's strategies as she works with a Guided Reading group.

Guided Reading Format

Format Outline
1. Story introduction
2. Picture walk
3. First reading
4. Second reading
5. Discussion
6. Mini language lesson
7. Independent practice or follow-up activity

1. Story introduction

(The teacher has the only copy of the book.)
▶ Give students the title and have them predict what the story might be about by using the cover and title page illustrations.

2. Picture walk

(The teacher has the only copy of the book.)
▶ Implant important or new language found in the story.
▶ Highlight the key concepts of the story.
▶ Evaluate the students' prior knowledge of the story topic and look for ways to connect the children with the story.

3. First reading

(The teacher has the only copy of the book.)
▶ Model the language pattern by reading the first two or three pages of the story.
▶ Use the cloze technique as you read through the rest of the story to allow students to take over as much of the reading as possible.
▶ Begin developing strategy awareness in students by referring to or modeling the use of picture clues, visual clues, structure clues, and the meaning of the story. Leave several opportunities for the children to use reading strategies.
▶ Prompt and praise the successful use of strategies as you work with the children.

4. Second reading

(Each child has a copy of the book.)

▶ Have the children read the story orally together. However, allow each child to read the story at his or her own pace, attempting to use reading strategies when appropriate.

▶ Guide and observe the children as they read. Evaluate their use of concepts of print and word knowledge.

▶ Prompt and praise the successful use of strategies.

5. Discussion

▶ Discuss topics, ideas, and literary elements of the story with the children. Focus on meaning.

▶ Relate the story to the children's lives whenever possible.

▶ Give students the opportunity to retell the story.

6. Mini language lesson

▶ A mini language lesson can take place at any point in the Guided Reading process where it is applicable and is based on the needs of the students.

▶ A mini language lesson at this level can focus on highlighting concepts of print, sight words, and/or the beginning use of strategies.

7. Independent practice or follow-up activity

▶ Students can read the new book independently.

▶ Follow-up activities should focus on a concept found in the book. Follow-up activities should be done only occasionally, perhaps once or twice a week. The Guided Reading activity booklets contain ideas for follow-up activities relating to each book.

Strategy Prompts for the Early Emergent Level

Focus on directionality

- Where do you start reading?
- Put your finger on the first word.
- Which way do you go?
- Now where do you go?
- Can you find the title page?
- Point to the title.

Focus on one-to-one correspondence

- Point to the words and read.
- Read it with your finger.
- Did that match?
- Were there enough words?

Focus on locating known words

- Can you point to _____?
- Show me _____.
- How did you know?

Focus on locating unknown words

- What would you expect to see in the word _____?
- Can you find _____?
- How did you know that word was _____?

FOCUS ON CONCEPTS OF PRINT

Huggles' Breakfast by Joy Cowley (SUNSHINE Level 1, Set A)

The main purpose of the following early emergent Guided Reading is to focus on certain concepts of print, such as reading text versus pictures, reading from left to right, and pointing to words to indicate one-to-one correspondence of spoken and written words. Elements of stories are also examined (for example, happy endings versus sad endings).

In this example, the teacher confines the picture walk to the cover, the title page, and

pages 2–3 of the text. Then she begins the first reading on page 2. In this way, the teacher has combined steps 1 and 2 of the early emergent Guided Reading format. This is a common variation of the format.

The mini language lesson involves the concept of "first" (first page, first word) and the word *a*, which appears throughout the text. (In the Guided Reading models, *T* stands for *teacher*, *C* for *child*, *T&C* for *teacher and children*, and *All* for *all children*.)

STORY INTRODUCTION AND PICTURE WALK
(The teacher has the only copy of the book.)
The teacher begins by holding up a copy of the book and asking open-ended questions about the cover.

▼ **cover**
T: *(Pointing to Huggles on the cover.)*
This is a very special guy! What can you tell me about him?
C: He's purple.
C: He's funny.
C: He's got big feet...and yellow eyes.
T: What else do you see in the picture?
C: A carrot.
C: A cake.
C: A bone.
C: A fish.
T: What do you think he is going to do in this story?

A carrot, / a cake,

a fish, / a bone,

a banana, / a sausage, / a telephone.

C: He looks like he's eating.

C: He looks hungry.

T: Do you know what he's eating? He's eating his breakfast. What do you have for breakfast?

C: Cereal.

Everyone, including the teacher, shares what they had for breakfast. In this way, the teacher is able to connect the children with the story line in a very personal, memorable way. Such discussion also helps set the focus and framework for predictions based upon personal experience as the story line unfolds.

▼ title page

T: Let's look at the title page. What does he have now?

C: A knife...and a fork.

C: He's getting ready to eat all those things.

T: The title of this story is *(pointing to the words)* Huggles' Breakfast.

Children at the early emergent level are drawn to pictures first. Indeed, many think the story is wholly in the pictures. Some children are unaware that the story actually appears as written text and that the text is at the bottom of the page. Therefore, the teacher starts the Guided Reading by focusing on the pictures. Once the children have gained the meaning they need from the pictures, the teacher then draws their attention to the text at the bottom of the page.

▼ page 2

T: *(Pointing to the picture.)* What's he eating here?

C: A carrot.

Notice that the question the teacher asks provides a natural response from the children—a response that is identical to the text. If the teacher had asked, "What's happening here?" she would have gotten a very different response, such as, "He's eating a carrot" or "He's got a carrot, and he's going to eat it." Notice how different these responses are from the actual text. In Guided Reading at this "rookie" level, we capitalize on the children's natural sense of oral language by asking questions that will guide them to match the text naturally in their responses.

▼ page 3

T: What does he have here?

C: A cake.

FIRST READING

(The teacher has the only copy of the book.)

▼ pages 2–3

T: Let's read our story and see what it says. *(Returning to pages 2–3 and pointing to the text as it is read.)* A carrot. A cake. *(Pointing to the bottom of page 3.)* What's this down here at the bottom of the picture?

C: A tail. It looks like a fish tail.

C: Oh, now he's going to eat a fish.

The artwork is designed to draw children's attention to the bottom of the picture through the placement of visual clues about what is going to happen on the next page. This feature will eventually direct the children's attention to the bottom of the page, where the text lies.

▼ pages 4–5

T: *(Reading.)* A...

C: Fish.

T: A...

C: Bone.

Notice how the teacher begins to use the cloze technique with the children. The first two pages establish the consistent language pattern in the children's minds. They now know where to get the clues for the text as it changes and what the sentence pattern is. They begin to take over the reading process.

▼ pages 6–7

T: *(Reading.)* A...

C: Banana.

T: *(Reading.)* A sausage.

Notice that the teacher does not wait for the children to come up with the word *sausage*. This is only one strategy that can be used in a situation where the children will probably not predict the word that appears in the text. An alternative strategy is to let the children respond and see if they get it. If their answer is "a hot dog," for example, then the teacher might say, "Yes, it looks like a hot dog, but this is something we eat for breakfast. What do you think it might be? A *sss...*"

A third strategy is to say, "Yes, it looks like a hot dog, but it starts with an *s*. Can you think of a word that might start with *sss?*" The teacher needs to be constantly sensitive to what the children know and how to elicit the most accurate response.

RING
RING!

T: *(Pointing to the phone.)* What's going on back here?
C: The phone's ringing.
T: How could you tell the phone's ringing?
C: 'Cause it has the noise marks on top.
T: What do you think he's going to do with the phone?
C: He's going to answer it.
C: He's going to order pizza.
C: He's going to invite some friends over. He eats a lot.
T: Well, let's turn the page and see. *(Turning the page and pausing.)*
C: Uh-oh!
(Laughter.)
C: He's eating the phone!
T: *(Pointing to the text.)* What do you think it says on this page? Let's read it together.
T&C: A telephone.
T: Did you like that story?
C: Yes.
T: Would you like to read it?
All: Yes!

SECOND READING
The children have been guided through the first reading, so they know the story line and meaning. They also know the repetitive writing structure. The success they experienced in responding to the cloze technique in the first reading has made them feel confident that they will now be able to read the story on their own.

(The teacher hands a copy of the book to each child.)

T: Put the book in front of you and point to the title.

Here, the teacher monitors the children's responses. If a child falters or is unsure, the teacher merely praises those children who have found the title to draw attention to the appropriate response.

T: Let's read the title together.
(The teacher monitors as the children point to the two words on their copies. The teacher points to the words on her own copy.)
T&C: *Huggles' Breakfast.*
T: Let's turn the page and read the title on the title page.
(The teacher monitors as the children locate the title, and she points to the two words as they read.)
T: Let's turn to where the story starts *(waiting to see them turn to page 2)* and begin reading the story.
T&C: *(Reading.)* A carrot.
T: Now read the whole story by yourself. Do you remember what you will do if you come to a word that you don't know?

Prior to independent reading, it is beneficial to have the children enumerate strategies for figuring out unknown words. This activity gives them a focus for their reading and reinforces what they should do when they encounter an unfamiliar word. At the early emergent level, you want to guide children to build their repertoire of strategies (for example, look at the pictures, start again, and so on). You can ask the children to list possible strategies to use or model or suggest the answers. As they gain expertise, their list of possible strategies will grow.

Independent reading is the ultimate goal of reading instruction. As the children first read the story, the teacher in this example overtly models strategies used by good readers: observing, predicting, using knowledge of initial sounds, and so forth. With this guidance, children learn to use the most appropriate reading strategies as they individually engage in the reading process.

The teacher then drops out of the reading, allowing the children to read together on their own. This is *not* a choral reading. Each child reads orally at his or her own pace, pointing to each word as he or she reads it. As the children read, the teacher continues to monitor pointing and directionality, any self-corrections that might occur, and knowledge of other early reading concepts. When the children have finished reading, the teacher might engage in a short conversation with them about the book.

DISCUSSION
T: Did you like that ending?
C: It was a good ending. It was funny.
T: How could it be a sad ending?
C: He might get a stomachache. His mom will be mad. They can't use the phone.

MINI LANGUAGE LESSON
T: Let's turn back to the first page of our story, where the story begins. *(Monitoring the children for the concepts of "first" and where the actual story begins as opposed to the title page.)* That's right, page 2. Let's read the page together.
T&C: A carrot.
T: Can you put your fingers around the first word? *(Monitors.)* What little word is that?
C: *A.*
T: What excellent readers you are! You know the word *A.* Good job!

FOLLOW-UP ACTIVITY
The teacher could then introduce a follow-up activity. It might be making a shopping list to buy the items the children would like to have for breakfast, illustrating on a white paper plate what they would like for breakfast, or doing both, depending on the developmental level of the children. They do not always need a follow-up activity in another content area (such as math, science, or social studies). Doing an extensive follow-up after every Guided Reading is not necessary.

One of the best follow-ups is simply to have the children pair up and read the story to each other. Any other follow-up activities should be meaningful and authentic and should relate naturally to the story. Ideally, follow-up activities have a practical purpose and/or make a useful contribution to the class reading resources.

Model 2

FOCUS ON CONCEPTS OF PRINT

Hello by Joy Cowley
(THE STORY BOX® Level 1, Set D)

The purpose of this Guided Reading is to focus on one-to-one correspondence, story sense, print concepts, and reading strategies. In the first reading, the teacher guides the children through the text in several ways:

- By familiarizing them with the story content and meaning

- By guiding them to observe the pictures in a way that supplies specific clues to the text

- By providing them with an oral experience of the sound of the language and the repetitive structure of the sentence pattern

- By using the cloze technique (pausing while the children make predictions) to guide them to supply the text on several occasions

The mini language lesson involves the concepts of letter identification and of upper- and lowercase letters.

STORY INTRODUCTION

(The teacher has the only copy of the book.)

▼ **cover**

T: Let's look at the front cover. What can you see in the picture?

C: A cat.
C: Some fish.
C: A lion.
C: Two cats.
T: *(Opening the book to show the entire cover illustration.)* What about here on the back cover?
C: Turkeys.
C: Donkeys.
C: And some dogs.
T: What is the turkey looking at?
C: Another turkey.
T: What about the fish?
C: The other fish.
T: What do you think they might be saying to each other?
All: *(Many answers.)*

▼ **title page**

T: Who's here, on the title page?
C: A boy.
C: And a girl.
T: And what do people say when they meet each other?
C: Hi.
C: Hello.
T: *(Pointing to the title.)* Well, that's the title of our story—*Hello.*
T: Let's look back at the cover. Do any of the animals look like they might be saying hello?
C: The dogs.

A donkey says to a donkey, "Hee-haw, hee-haw."
2

A lion says to a lion, "Roar, roar, roar."
3

A dog says to a dog, "Bow, wow, wow."
4

A cat says to a cat, "Me-ow, me-ow, me-ow."
5

A turkey says to a turkey, "Gobble, gobble, gobble."
6

A fish says to a fish, "Bubble, bubble, bubble."
7

I say to the people I know, "Hello, hello, hello."
8

T: How do you think they might say hello?

C: Woof, woof!

T: Are there any others?

All: *(Many similar responses.)*

T: What do you think our story will be about?

C: The animals all talking to each other.

C: They all meet each other.

T: Those are both good guesses. Let's see what our story says. *(Pointing to the title.)* The title is *Hello,* and it's written by Joy Cowley.

PICTURE WALK

(The teacher has the only copy of the book.)

▼ **pages 2–3**

T: *(Pointing to the donkey.)* What's this?

C: A donkey.

Note that the teacher states the question so that the children answer with a phrase that is close to the text. If the teacher had asked, "What do you see in the picture?" the children might have answered "donkeys" or "two donkeys."

T: Who knows what kind of a noise a donkey might make?

C: Hee-haw, hee-haw.

T: *(Pointing to the lion with its mouth open.)* And who's talking here?

C: A lion.

T: What sound might a lion make?

C: Roar!

C: G-r-r-r-r.

The teacher could continue through the whole story using only the pictures to guide the children's responses. This technique is especially valuable for the most inexperienced readers or for children for whom English is a second language. The teacher in this model, however, chooses to use the pictures for only the first two pages so that the children get a general sense of the story before turning their attention to the text. Even as children begin to supply the text in this cloze example, the teacher continues to clearly point to each word.

FIRST READING

(The teacher has the only copy of the book.)

▼ **pages 2–3**

T: *(Reading and pointing to the text on pages 2–3 as one unit to emphasize the rhyme.)* A donkey says to a donkey, "Hee-haw, hee-haw." A lion says to a lion, "Roar, roar, roar."

▼ **page 4**

T: A... *(cloze pause)*
C: dog...
T: says to a...
C: dog...
T: "Bow, wow, wow."

▼ **page 5**

T: A...
C: cat...
T: says...
C: to a cat...
T: "Me-ow...
T&C: ...me-ow, me-ow."

▼ **page 6**

T: A...
C: turkey...
T: says...
C: to a turkey...
T&C: "Gobble, gobble, gobble."

▼ **page 7**

T: A...
C: fish says to a fish...
T: "Bubble, bubble, bubble."

▼ **page 8**

T: I say to the people I know, "Hello...
C: ...hello, hello."
T: Was that a funny story?
C: Yes!
T: Let's go back and read the whole story now.

SECOND READING

The early emergent level books are designed to foster independence and support instant reading. Initially, the guidance strategies in Guided Reading focus on the recognition and use of those features that provide support. Prior to the second reading, the teacher uses a common strategy that begins to focus children on the use of reading strategies. The number of strategies available to the children increases as they gain control of the reading process.

For the second reading, each child has a copy of the book, and the teacher asks the children to read aloud on their own while she monitors and evaluates their progress. If a particular teaching point is to be made within the body of the text, the teacher should usually allow the children to have an uninterrupted reading before going back to focus on a specific point.

(Each child has a copy of the book.)
T: Let's turn to the title page and read the title.
T&C: *Hello.*
T: Let's read who wrote this story.
T&C: *By Joy Cowley.*
T: Turn to page 2, and go ahead and read the story. *(Reading.)* A donkey says to a donkey, "Hee-haw, hee-haw." *(Addresses the group.)* Now read the whole story silently by yourself. Do you remember what to do if you come to a word that you don't know?
(The teacher then asks the children to enumerate the different strategies they know how to use.)

Prior to independent reading, it is beneficial to have the children discuss strategies for unknown words. This discussion gives them a focus for their reading and reinforces what strategies to use when they encounter an unfamiliar word. One way to discuss these strategies is by listing them on a chart. You can check off the strategies that the children list and then choose a new one to model for the children. Add to the list of potential strategies as the children progress in their reading development.

Independent reading is the ultimate goal of reading instruction. As the children first read the story, the teacher in this example overtly models strategies used by good readers: observing, predicting, using knowledge of initial sounds, and so forth. With this guidance, chil-dren learn to use the most appropriate reading strategies as they individually engage in the reading process.

At this point, the teacher withdraws from participation and allows the children to proceed on their own. The children read through the story orally together (but not necessarily in unison), pointing to each word as they read. The teacher observes, listens, monitors, and evaluates each child during this oral reading.

MINI LANGUAGE LESSON

The teacher uses the cover of this story to focus on some basic print concepts and letter-sound knowledge.
T: Show me where the title is. *(Monitors responses.)* Let's read the title together.
T&C: *Hello.*
T: Put your finger on either side of the first letter. Who can tell me the name of that letter or what sound it makes?
C: *H.*
T: Is it a capital *H* or a lowercase *h?*
C: Capital *H.*
T: Why is there a capital *H* here?
C: Because it's the title.
T: Can you find another *h* in the story?
(Several children find various examples and discuss whether they are capital H *or lower-case* h.*)*

The teacher monitors and evaluates the children's knowledge during this time by observing their responses.

DISCUSSION AND FOLLOW-UP ACTIVITY

The teacher introduces a discussion on the ways different animals and people greet each other. She invites the children to brainstorm to create a chart of other animals and the sounds they make when "saying hello." As a follow-up activity for this story, the teacher asks the children to draw the animals in the book and then add speech bubbles that show how the animals say hello.

Note that it is not necessary to do an extensive follow-up activity with every book. Any follow-up activities should be meaningful and authentic and should relate naturally to the story. It is also effective to have children do paired reading at this time.

Chapter 3

Upper Emergent Level

This chapter gives two suggested formats for Guided Reading at the upper emergent level and two models of Guided Reading sessions. For each format, an outline of the basic Guided Reading process is followed by a more detailed description of each step of the format.

After the format is explained, a Guided Reading model follows. Each model includes a transcript of an actual classroom Guided Reading session and explanations of or comments on the teacher's strategies as she works with a Guided Reading group.

Guided Reading Format 1
Focus on strategies
(optional hidden text)

Format 1 Outline

1. Story introduction
2. Picture walk
3. Strategy reminder
4. First reading
5. Strategy reinforcer
6. Discussion
7. Second reading (paired reading)
8. Mini language lesson
9. Independent practice or follow-up activity

1. Story introduction

(The teacher has the only copy of the book.)

▶ Give students the title and have them predict what the story might be about by using the cover and title page illustrations.

2. Picture walk

(The teacher has the only copy of the book.)

▶ Highlight the key concepts of the story.
▶ Develop a cognitive web on a chart or through discussion to link students' prior knowledge to the new book.
▶ Reinforce the use of reading strategies by implanting unusual language structures.
▶ You may choose to hide the text in the story with your hand during this reading, allowing students to focus on getting meaning from the illustrations. Covering the text also gives students the opportunity to use their own strategies when they read the book for the first time.

3. Strategy reminder

▶ Elicit from the students possible reading strategies that they might need to use while reading the book.

4. First reading

(Each child has a copy of the book.)

▶ Have the students read the story orally together. However, allow each child to read the story at his or her own pace, practicing reading strategies when appropriate.
▶ Prompt and praise the successful use of strategies as you observe and/or work with each student.

5. Strategy reinforcer

▶ Encourage students to discuss how they knew what strategies to use. You might ask, "How did you know that word was _____?" or "What could you have done to figure out that word?"

▶ Have students share what they did to solve print problems.

▶ Reinforce the correct use or attempted use of strategies.

6. Discussion

▶ Discuss the literary elements of the story.

▶ Relate the story to the children's lives whenever possible.

▶ Give students the opportunity to retell the story.

7. Second reading (paired reading)

▶ Have students read with a partner to practice fluency.

8. Mini language lesson

▶ A mini language lesson can take place at any point in the Guided Reading process where it is applicable and is based on the needs of the students.

▶ A mini language lesson at this level can focus on strategy development, print features, vocabulary, literary elements, and/or language structures.

9. Independent practice or follow-up activity

▶ Students can read the new book independently, read from their book baskets of familiar books, or read materials at reading centers.

▶ Follow-up activities should focus on a concept found in the book. Follow-up activities should be done only occasionally, perhaps once or twice a week. The Guided Reading activity booklets contain ideas for follow-up activities relating to each book.

Strategy Prompts for the Upper Emergent Level

Focus on meaning cues

- Did that make sense?
- Look at the pictures.
- What happened in the story when _____?
- What do you think it might be?

Focus on structure cues

- Did that sound right?
- Can you reread that?
- Can you say that another way?
- What is another word that might fit here?

Focus on visual cues

- Does that look right?
- What letter/sound does it start/end with?

- What would you expect to see at the beginning/in the middle/at the end?
- Do you know another word that might start/end with those letters?
- Can you get your mouth ready to say that word/sound?

Focus on self-correcting

- There is a difficult [or "tricky"] part here. Can you find it?
- Are you right? Could that be _____?
- Take a closer look at _____.
- How did you know that this word was _____?

Focus on cross-checking

- How did you know that was _____?
- Is there another way to tell?
- It could be _____, but look at _____.

Model 1

FOCUS ON STRATEGIES (optional hidden text)

Stop! by Joy Cowley
(THE STORY BOX Level 1, Set E)

At the beginning of the upper emergent level, children may still need some supportive picture cues and guidance from the teacher. In this Guided Reading model, the teacher focuses on the use of reading strategies and initial letter combinations. Children are encouraged to verbalize the cues and strategies that they use with unfamiliar words.

To maximize the use of strategies, the teacher covers up the text when doing the picture walk. Then when the children see the text for the first time, they can really use what they know about applying strategies. Notice that the teacher in this example exposes the text on pages 8–9 to model how the children might figure out an unknown word. The same kind of problem occurs on pages 10–11, but the teacher leaves it for the children to figure out on their own in the first reading. The mini language lesson in this example focuses on the concept of initial letter combinations and increasing language development. (In the Guided Reading models, *T* stands for *teacher*, *C* for *child*, *T&C* for *teacher and children*, and *All* for *all children*.)

STORY INTRODUCTION AND PICTURE WALK
(The teacher has the only copy of the book.)
At this point, the teacher has the only copy of the book so that the children's attention is focused on the teacher. The teacher covers the text with her hand as she goes through the pictures.

▼ **cover**
T: *(Holding up the book.)* What do you think that this story might be about?
C: A milkman.
T: Anything else?
C: Milk bottles.

▼ **title page**
T: Let's look at the title page and see if you can get any more ideas of what the book is about.
C: A cat.
T: Does anyone know the title of the story?
C: *Stop!*

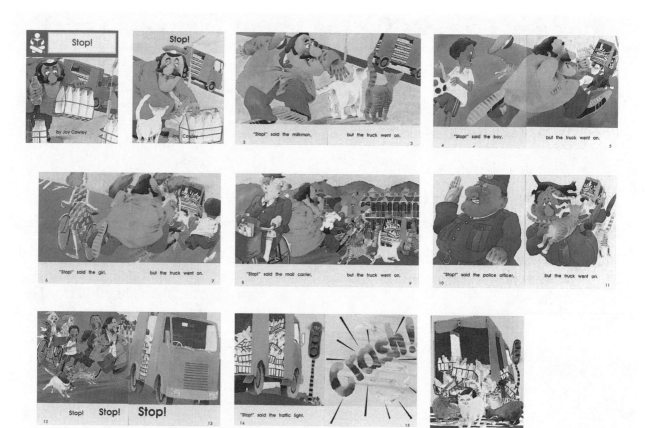

T: That's right. The title is *Stop!* What do you suppose is going to have to stop?
C: The milkman.
C: The cat.

▼ **pages 2–3**
T: Let's look at the pictures to see what the story is going to be about. Oh, no! What is everyone looking at?
C: The milk truck.
T: Why are they looking at the milk truck?
C: It looks like it's moving.
T: How can you tell that the milk truck is moving?
C: The wiggly lines by the truck mean it's moving.

Notice how the teacher draws attention to the motion lines in the illustrations to reinforce the use of picture cues.

T: What do you think the milkman said when he saw the truck moving?
All: Stop!
T: Did the truck stop?
All: No.

T: No, it just went on, didn't it?

Note that the teacher has implanted the language *(went on)* at this point because of the unfamiliar pattern in this story.

▼ **pages 4–5**
T: Turn to page 4. Who is yelling "Stop!" on this page?
C: The boy.
T: But the truck went on, didn't it?

▼ **pages 6–7**
T: Who wants the truck to stop here?
C: The girl.

▼ **pages 8–9**
T: Who is yelling "Stop!" on page 8?
C: The mailman.
T: What would be another way to say *mailman?*
C: Postman.
T: Look at the last two words on this page. *(Holding the book and exposing the text so that the whole group has an opportunity to see the words.)* Could this say *postman?*
C: No.

T: Why can't it be *postman?*
C: There's no *p* and no *man.*
T: What could it be then? Let's read this page together. *(The teacher points to the words as she shows the book to the group and all read together.)*
All: "Stop!" said the mail c...
(Children pause. This is not a familiar word for many children so the teacher has elected to give the word to the children.)
T: Could he be the mail carrier?
C: Yes.
T: How will you remember that this says mail carrier?
C: *Carrier* starts with a *c.*
T: Nice job of looking at the beginning sound.

Notice that the teacher encourages the children to verbalize the strategies and cue systems used in figuring out unknown words. She focuses on visual cues since the children's first responses of *mailman* and *postman* made sense and sounded right in the story.

▼ pages 10–11
T: Oh, oh! Who's telling the truck to stop now?
C: The policeman.

The teacher doesn't stop to point out this error (*policeman* instead of *police officer*) as many of the students will be able to use their own strategies during independent reading to figure it out.

▼ pages 12–13
T: What else is chasing the truck?
C: Lots of cats.
C: All the people.
T: What do you think might happen to the milk truck?
C: It might stop.
C: It will get a ticket from the policeman.
C: It might crash.
T: Let's turn the page and find out what happens.

▼ pages 14–15
T: Did the truck stop for the traffic light?
All: No!
C: It crashed!
T: Oh, dear! Will the milkman and everyone be unhappy?
C: Yes.
T: Turn to the last page to find out.

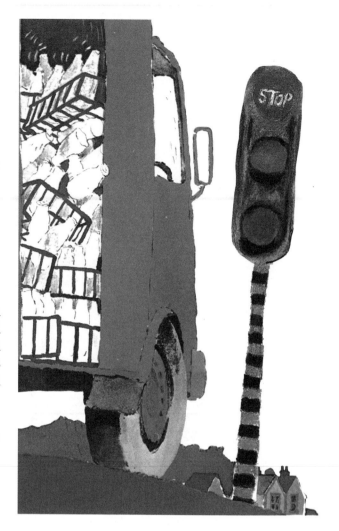

▼ page 16
T: Was everyone unhappy?
C: No. The cats were very happy.

STRATEGY REMINDER AND FIRST READING
(Each child has a copy of the book.)
The upper emergent level books are designed to increase independent reading skills. For this first reading, each child has his or her own copy of the book. If a particular teaching point is to be made within the body of the text, the teacher should usually allow children to have an uninterrupted reading before going back to focus on a specific point.
T: Now we'll read the whole story together. Do you remember what to do if you come to a word that you don't know?
(The children list various strategies they can use to figure out unfamiliar words. Then they go on to read the story simultaneously out loud.)

STRATEGY REINFORCER, DISCUSSION, AND SECOND READING (PAIRED READING)

The teacher and the children discuss the strategies that the children used to solve print problems. The teacher then guides the children into a brief discussion about the story. The children then reread the story with partners to practice fluency.

MINI LANGUAGE LESSON AND FOLLOW-UP ACTIVITY

T: Let's look at the word *stop*. What do you see at the beginning of *stop*?

C: *S*.

C: *St*.

T: Right. *Stop* starts with an *st* blend. Slide your finger under the word *stop* and look at the *st* blend.

(Children slide finger under the word. This sliding helps them to focus on the whole word.)

T: *Stop* is a really important word in our everyday lives. Let's think of some people, things, or animals that might tell us to stop and why we should stop for them.

(The teacher keeps track of their brainstorming on a list with people/animals/ things, how they tell us to stop, and why we should stop.)

C: A stop sign.

T: Why should we stop for a stop sign?

C: To watch for traffic and cars.

T: Good. What else?

C: The crossing guard at school tells us to wait for cars.

C: The tape recorder tells us to stop the tape at the end.

C: My mom is always telling me to stop doing something.

(Laughter.)

The teacher adds the children's suggestions to the list. The children can then each select one thing to write about and illustrate that tells about stopping.

You do not have to do an extensive follow-up activity with every book. Any follow-up activities should be meaningful and authentic and should relate naturally to the story. It is also effective to have children do paired reading at this time.

3

Guided Reading Format 2

Focus on silent Guided Reading

This format is provided as a brief transition to conducting Guided Reading at the early fluency level. The majority of upper emergent Guided Reading time is spent using Format 1, which focuses on group oral reading.

Teachers should not move children into silent Guided Reading until the children are confident in their use of strategies. The length of time spent on this transition phase will vary depending on the needs of the children in the group. This period may range from a few days to several weeks.

Format 2 Outline

1. Story introduction
2. Picture walk
3. First reading
   *Focus questions
4. Second reading
5. Discussion
6. Mini language lesson
7. Independent practice or follow-up activity

1. Story introduction

(The teacher has the only copy of the book.)

▶ Involve the students in figuring out the title of the story.
▶ Discuss the cover illustrations.
▶ Implant any new or difficult words or language patterns.
▶ Help students develop a cognitive web on a chart or through discussion to link their prior knowledge to the book.

2. Picture walk

(The teacher has the only copy of the book.)

▶ Involve students in predicting the story line through the pictures.
▶ Highlight the key concepts of the story.
▶ Reinforce the use of reading strategies by implanting unusual language structures.
▶ You may choose to hide the text in the story with your hand during this reading, allowing the students to focus on getting meaning from the illustrations. Covering the text also gives students the opportunity to use their own strategies when they read the book for the first time.
▶ Elicit from the students possible reading strategies that they might need to use while reading the book.

3. First reading

(Each child has a copy of the book.)
   * Focus questions
▶ Ask focus questions for every two to four pages of the story.
▶ Guide the students to read silently to find the answers to these questions.
▶ Have the students orally confirm their answers to focus questions by locating the appropriate text that supports their answers.

- Continue through the story using this format.
- Encourage children to discuss print problems and solutions. Ask the children to discuss how they knew what strategies to use. You might ask, "How did you know that word was _____?" or "What could you have done to figure out that word?"

4. Second reading

- Have the children silently read the whole story as you observe and assist with strategy development and reinforcement as necessary.
- You might reread the story or portions of the story again with the students, providing a fluent model for them to hear.

5. Discussion

- Discuss the literary elements found in the story.
- Relate the story to the children's lives whenever possible.
- Give students the opportunity to retell the story.

6. Mini language lesson

- A mini language lesson can take place at any point in the Guided Reading process where it is applicable and is based on the needs of the students.
- A mini language lesson at this level can focus on strategy development, print features, vocabulary, literary elements, and/or language structures.

7. Independent practice or follow-up activity

- Students can read the new book independently, read from their book baskets of familiar books, or read materials at reading centers.
- Follow-up activities should focus on a concept found in the book. Follow-up activities should be done only occasionally, perhaps once or twice a week. The Guided Reading activity booklets contain ideas for follow-up activities relating to each book.

3

Strategy Prompts for the Upper Emergent Level

Focus on meaning cues
- Did that make sense?
- Look at the pictures.
- What happened in the story when _____?
- What do you think it might be?

Focus on structure cues
- Did that sound right?
- Can you reread that?
- Can you say that another way?
- What is another word that might fit here?

Focus on visual cues
- Does that look right?
- What letter/sound does it start/end with?

- What would you expect to see at the beginning/in the middle/at the end?
- Do you know another word that might start/end with those letters?
- Can you get your mouth ready to say that word/sound?

Focus on self-correcting
- There is a difficult [or "tricky"] part here. Can you find it?
- Are you right? Could that be _____?
- Take a closer look at _____.
- How did you know that this word was _____?

Focus on cross-checking
- How did you know that was _____?
- Is there another way to tell?
- It could be _____, but look at _____.

(This chart is the same as that given on page 25.)

Model 2

FOCUS ON SILENT GUIDED READING

Noise by Joy Cowley
(SUNSHINE Level 1, Set G)

In this Guided Reading, done with a first-grade group, the teacher guides the children away from oral reading and toward silent reading. The focus is on meaning as the teacher uses the pictures to walk through the story prior to reading it. The teacher does the picture walk. The first reading is done with the children reading silently and then discussing concepts and language as they progress through the story.

STORY INTRODUCTION

(The teacher has the only copy of the book.)

▼ **cover**

T: Now, we've been talking about different sounds today. And the story we are going to read is about different sounds. Can you see anything in the picture on the cover that would be making different sounds?

C: There are car sounds.

C: And a motorcycle.

C: A dog.

C: People sounds.

C: Roller skates.

T: *(Pointing to earphones.)* What's this?

C: It's something you hear with.

T: Do you know what it's called?

C: It's when you don't hear any noise outside, only on the inside.

T: Inside your ear; that's right.

C: A radio.

C: A Walkman.

T: That's right, a Walkman. Let's look at the title. See if you can tell me what it says.

C: It says *Noise*.

T: How did you know it said *Noise*?

C: Because it's got an *n* and an *s*.

The teacher reinforces and draws attention to the use of effective strategies that children may or may not be using consciously.

PICTURE WALK

(The teacher has the only copy of the book.)

T: Now we're going to have a look through the book before we actually read the story. We're going to use the pictures to help us know what the story will be about.

At this point, the teacher uses the illustrations to set up a cognitive framework for the story line and to create a web of understanding that will aid the children in predicting the words in the text. This activity gives the children a context in which to place information later, when they actually read through the story.

▼ title page

T: Now let's have a look at the title page. What's making noise on the title page?

C: The man drilling the ground.

T: What do these lines mean that the artist has drawn?

C: It means it's going really fast and tickly.

C: And his arms will be all jiggling up and down, too.

T: Yes. It's a very powerful tool, isn't it? What's he got on his ears?

C: Ear puffs.

T: That's nearly right. Not ear puffs, though, ear...

C: Muffs!

T: Right! Why do you think he has them on?

C: 'Cause his ears would hurt.

T: Do your ears hurt when you hear a very loud noise?

C: Yes, sometimes you get deaf.

▼ pages 2–4

T: I don't want you to read the story yet, just look at the pictures. What's making the noise in that picture?

(The teacher can choose to cover the text at this point if the children have several strategies and reading concepts in place.)

C: A radio.

T: Is that a particular sort of radio?

C: No.

T: Do you know what those radios are called when they have two big speakers like that?

C: I don't know.

C: A boom box.

T: *(Pointing to page 3.)* What about this picture? What is he listening to that's making a big noise?

C: A bop song.

T: A bop song. And what's that noise coming from?

C: The radio.

T: From a radio. It's a special kind of radio. It does lots more things.

C: It's just a radio.

T: Well, we'll see when we read our story.

Notice that the teacher doesn't press for specialized terms at this point. Later, the children will use their sense of meaning in combination with their sense of the grammatical structure of the text and visual letter clues to figure out any unknown words.

The emphasis at this stage in Guided Reading is on providing opportunities for the children to use a variety of strategies to solve print problems as they read the story. However, the challenging words must be no more than 5 percent of the text in order for the children to be able to use their strategies effectively.

T: What are they looking at here?

C: TV.

C: Video.

T: Yes. Now what do you think it would be like if all those things were on in the house at the same time?

C: A very loud noise.

C: All different noises.

T: How would you feel if you were listening to all of these noises?

C: My ears will hurt.

T: How would you feel?

C: I'd just feel like I was deaf.

▼ pages 4–5

T: Look at the mother. Does she like listening to all those noises together?

C: No, because she's got a funny face.

T: A funny face? Why do you think she's got her hand out like that?

All: Stop!

C: And she's thirsty, too.

▼ pages 6–7

T: Well, *now* how does Mom look?

C: Happy.

T: What do you think happened?

C: They turned them all off.

▼ pages 8–9

T: Now where are they?

C: Outside.

C: On the little porch.

C: On the deck.

T: And what sort of house do they live in?

C: There's a house for everyone.

T: What kind of building is this?

C: An apartment.

T: Why do you think she took them outside?
C: To listen to the noises outside.
T: Would you be able to hear any noise? Take a look at the picture. Can you see anything that might be making a noise?
C: A person drilling.
C: A cat and a dog might be meowing and barking.
T: What else might be making a noise in that picture?
C: The wind.
C: The man might be shouting to someone.
T: Do you think they could hear all those noises when they had all those stereos and radios on?
All: No.
T: When they first went out on the porch, do you think they could hear anything at first, after they had been listening to those very loud noises?
C: No.
C: Yes.

▼ pages 10–11
T: Let's have a look at the next page. Now what are they doing?
C: They are looking at all the things that are noisy.

T: How can you tell that?
C: 'Cause they are pointing.
T: What's making all the different noises? (Various responses.)
T: What noises would be the very loudest?
C: The ambulance.
T: What sort of sound would that make? (A child wails like a siren to imitate the noise.)
C: The saw.
T: And what sound would be not quite so loud?
C: The cars.
T: At first, they were listening to sounds that were very loud, like the radio and TV. Then their mom took them outside, and they listened to sounds that were not quite so loud.

▼ pages 12–13
T: Let's turn the page and look at what they notice next.
C: A bird.
C: A bee.
C: Drip...drop...drip.
T: What kind of sounds are they listening to now? Instead of big sounds, they are listening to very...
C: Little sounds.

▼ **pages 14–15**

T: But then what did they do?

C: They started being noisy again.

T: What's that big radio thing called? You still haven't told me yet.

C: It's just an old radio.

T: Well, in the story you might find that it has another name.

▼ **page 16**

T: And how does it end?

C: They're all dancing.

T: We're going to read our story now, but first I'm going to give you a little pattern that you'll find in the story. If we do it together now, it will help you read it when we get to that part. This is how it goes. Watch me do it first and then we'll do it together. *(The teacher alternates clapping thighs and hands while chanting.)* Yukka-dukka, yukka-dukka, yah-yah-yah! *(The teacher and children chant these lines twice, with the children mimicking the teacher's clapping motions.)*

FIRST READING, FOCUS QUESTIONS, AND MINI LANGUAGE LESSONS

(Each child has a copy of the book.)

Notice that here the teacher incorporates mini language lessons into the first reading. These mini language lessons focus on the names of the children in the story and on identifying dialogue within quotation marks. Mini language lessons can be incorporated into any step of the Guided Reading process where appropriate or based on the group's needs.

T: Let's look at the cover and read the title together.

T&C: *Noise.*

T: Oh, what good, loud voices. Let's read the title on the title page, too.

C: *Noise.*

▼ **pages 2–3**

T: Good. Now, remembering that pattern of the yukka-dukka chant, I want you to read the first two pages to yourself, in your head, and don't worry if you're not sure what the names are, because we'll work them out later. When you're done reading, just sit up so I'll know you're finished.

(All the children read pages 2–3 silently.)

Notice how the teacher focuses the children's attention on the meaning of the story in two ways. First, the teacher teaches the children the chant that they will encounter on this page so that they will have the sound of the language for this unusual text ringing in their ears when they come to it. Second, they are told not to worry about the names, because they will work them out together if they need to when they've finished reading the pages.

Some children have more ability to read silently than others. Some read with a soft whisper. The teacher may use special "silent" signals to help the children remember to read with their eyes.

(After beginning to read the chant during the first reading, one child exclaims, "It's in there!" When the children show they are finished, the teacher goes on with focus questions for every few pages of the story.)

T: OK. Let's begin with the characters' names.

C: I know what his name is.

C: So do I.

T: Does anyone know the name of the girl on page 2?

C: Julie.

T: Good. And what about the boy on the next page? It's quite a different sort of name, isn't it? How does it start?

C: *B.*

C: It begins with a *b* and an *r.*

T: So it begins like Brian. Can you think of another name like Brian?

C: Brendan.

T: Yes, but this name is not Brendan. You're nearly right. Look at the end of it.

(Different attempts are made.)

C: Brent!

T: That's right! Will you read that page?

C: Brent had the stereo on. Yukka-dukka, yukka-dukka, yah-yah-yah!

T: So now you've found out the name of the big radio with the two speakers. It's a...

C: Stereo!

C: They were listening to the radio and a stereo.

C: We've got a stereo at home.

T: What's the yukka-dukka mean?

C: That's just the music.

C: The different sounds that it's making.

▼ **pages 4–5**

T: Good. Now read the next two pages in your mind, please.

(Children signal when they have finished reading.)

T: Good. Did you all know the boy's name on that page?

C: Jason.

T: That's right—Jason. And what did Mom do?

C: She got mad at all the noise.

T: And what did she say?

C: "Stop that noise!" Mom yelled.

T: What was just the part that Mom said?

C: "Stop that noise!"

The teacher again helps to clarify any confusion surrounding the difference between the full text and just the dialogue.

▼ **pages 6–7**

T: Try reading the next two pages in your mind to see what happens.

(Children read silently.)

C: They turned it all off.

T: And how did Mom feel?

C: Better.

T: What did she actually say? Put your fingers around the part that she said and read it.

C: *(Reading.)* "That's better."

▼ **pages 8–9**

T: *(After silent reading.)* So what did Mom do?

C: She took them outside.

T: Why did she do that?

C: So they could listen.

T: Put your fingers around the part that tells you what they heard. What did they hear?

C: Nothing.

T: What did Jason say?

C: "Not a thing."

T: Not a thing. What does that mean?

C: Nothing.

T: That's right. It means the same as nothing. But Mom told them to keep on...

C: Listening.

Notice how the teacher draws the children's attention to the subtle variation in text that the author chose to use while still retaining the same meaning.

▼ **pages 10–11**

T: Read the pages with your eyes and put your hand up when you can tell me one thing that they heard that's in the story.

(Children read silently.)

T: What is one thing that they heard?

C: Cars.

(Other children begin to interrupt with ambulance; the teacher stops them and calls on the child with a hand up.)

C: An ambulance.

T: Yes, and who can tell me just one other thing they heard?

C: A saw.

T: What noise do you think was the loudest?

C: The saw.

T: It could be the saw. Why do you think that?

C: Because it's right near their ears.

T: Yes, it could be. Does anyone else have an idea of what might be the loudest?

C: It could be the ambulance.

T: And why do you think that?

C: 'Cause it's louder than everything.

C: It has to be louder, so you can always hear it.

T: Yes, that's true, it's very important that we hear it, isn't it?

▼ **pages 12–13**

T: Now let's read the next two pages. And when you've finished reading, I'd like you to put your fingers around the smallest sound.

(Children begin reading.)

When all the children have put their fingers around one of the words, the teacher finds three children with different answers to call upon. Focusing on more than one right answer helps to promote and support a range of thinking and allows a variety of opinions to be honored.

T: What have you got your fingers around?

C: I put it around a bumblebee.

T: What have you got your fingers around?

C: The water.

T: What do you think?

C: The bird.

T: What kind of sounds are all these sounds?

C: Just very little sounds.

C: You don't really hear them very much.

▼ **pages 14–15**

T: Now read the next page silently and tell me what happened.

(Children read silently.)

C: They did it all over again.

T: Do you think they turned them up as loud?

C: No.

▼ **page 16**

T: Let's turn the page and read the last page together.

T&C: Yukka-dukka, yukka-dukka, yah-yah-yah!

T: Well, do you think they turned it up loud or not?

C: Yes.

T: Did you like that story?

C: I think it was good.

T: Why?

C: Because of all the noises I hear.

C: They would make my ears hurt.

C: I liked the loud noises.

C: My dad has a buzz saw.

SECOND READING

The children read the book silently for the second reading. The teacher interacts with members of the group as needed.

DISCUSSION AND FOLLOW-UP ACTIVITY

The teacher suggests making a Big Book of loud sounds and a little book of soft sounds. She brainstorms with the children things that make loud sounds and things that make soft sounds. They are given a big sheet of paper on which to draw something that makes a big sound and a small sheet of paper to draw something that makes a quiet sound. The pictures are then pasted into two separate books called "Loud Sounds" and "Soft Sounds."

You do not have to do an extensive follow-up activity with every book. Any follow-up activities should be meaningful and authentic and should relate naturally to the story. It is also effective to have children do paired reading at this time.

3

Chapter 4

Early Fluency Level

This chapter gives two suggested formats for Guided Reading at the early fluency level and two models of Guided Reading sessions. For each format, an outline of the basic Guided Reading process is followed by a more detailed description of each step of the format.

After the format is explained, a Guided Reading model follows. Each model includes a transcript of an actual classroom Guided Reading session and explanations of and comments on the teacher's strategies as she works with a Guided Reading group. The second format and model focus on beginning literature circles. This is a transitional format to prepare students for literature circle discussions when they reach the fluency level.

Guided Reading Format 1
Focus on mastery of strategies and concepts of literature

Format 1 Outline
1. Story introduction
2. First reading
3. Second reading (optional)
4. Discussion
5. Mini language lesson
6. Follow-up activity

1. Story introduction
(Each child has a copy of the book.)
▶ Involve the students in figuring out the title and discuss the cover illustrations.

2. First reading
▶ Guide children to use a variety of strategies when reading. The focus at this level is on mastery of these strategies.
▶ Ask focus questions that encourage students to predict and confirm.
▶ Guide the students to read silently a specific section to find and confirm the literary elements of the story, such as character descriptions and plot lines.
▶ Continue through the story using this format.

3. Second reading (optional)
▶ Students can read the story again independently at their seats and/or respond in their journals.

Note: You may choose to do steps 4 and 5 the next day during Guided Reading time.

4. Discussion

▶ Discuss the literary elements found in the story.

▶ Relate the story to the children's lives whenever possible.

▶ Give students the opportunity to retell or react to the story.

5. Mini language lesson

▶ A mini language lesson can take place at any point in the Guided Reading process where it is applicable and is based on the needs of the students.

▶ A mini language lesson might include language structures or literary elements.

▶ A mini language lesson at this level can focus also on mastering reading strategies and using more than one strategy for cross-checking.

6. Follow-up activity

▶ Have the children begin responding to or reacting to the reading by using journal entries and/or doing other literature-related activities. The Guided Reading activity booklets contain ideas for follow-up activities relating to each book.

Strategy Prompts for the Early Fluency Level

Continue to focus on meaning, structure, and visual prompts from the upper emergent level.

✳Focus on self-correcting

- There is a difficult [or "tricky"] part here. Can you find it?
- Are you right? Could that be _____?
- Take a closer look at _____.
- How did you know that this word was _____?

✳Focus on cross-checking

- How did you know that was _____?
- Is there another way to tell?
- It could be _____, but look at _____.

✳Focus on self-monitoring

- Try that again.
- What did you notice?
- Were you right?
- How did you know?
- Why did you stop?

4

Model 1

FOCUS ON MASTERY OF STRATEGIES AND CONCEPTS OF LITERATURE

"Onion Soup" in *Tiddalik* (THE STORY BOX, Level 7)

In moving from the emergent levels to the early fluency level, the teacher guides the children to think about basic story conventions, such as plot structure, characters, and main ideas. Each child has a copy of the story for Guided Reading at this level.

Although some children continue to rely on the pictures to tell the story, the teacher guides them to look to the text for confirmation of their predictions and observations about the story line and characters. The children are familiar now with basic book conventions, such as the point at which one begins reading a page of text. They now focus more closely on the content of the text itself. (In the Guided Reading models, *T* stands for *teacher*, *C* for *child*, *T&C* for *teacher and children*, and *All* for *all children*.)

STORY INTRODUCTION

(Each child has a copy of the book.)
T: This story is about a woman named Mrs. Brown. She grows an enormous onion, and then finds out she's got a problem. I wonder what her problem might be?

C: She couldn't dig it up.
T: That could be her problem.
C: She's too big and she can't even bend over to dig it up.
T: That might be her problem. She makes onion soup with her onion. Have you ever made onion soup?
C: I have.
C: I love it!
T: You love it! Well. What did you use when you made onion soup? What did you put in it?
C: Onion!
T: Can you tell me what it tasted like?
C: Salt.
T: Anything else about it?
C: Too much onion.
T: Too much onion! Now we're going to find out what happened in the story and what Mrs. Brown's problem was.
C: I know what it is.
T: Do you?
C: She can't fit the onion in her house. It's too big.
T: It might be—that's a good idea. So as we read our story, think of this: What do you know about Mrs. Brown? And what do you think might happen next?

FIRST READING

T: Let's read, thinking of all these things as we read. Read to the bottom of page 3.
(All the children read.)

▼ pages 2–3

T: What do you know now about Mrs. Brown?

C: Well, I think she's trying to dig it [the onion] up.

T: Good. What could you say about her if she's trying hard to dig it up? What would you say about Mrs. Brown?

C: That it took her all day.

T: It did?

C: She dug all afternoon.

T: So would you say that she was hard-working?

C: Yes.

T: A hard-working woman. What else? Do you think she likes gardening?

C: Well, actually, she got tired of it.

T: Yes. So she must have worked very hard to get so tired.

C: Even though she dug it out with a bulldozer, it would still be hard because you might only get half of the onion out.

T: That's true. There's a lot of thinking she would have to do, wouldn't she?

C: And you wouldn't be able to get your arms around the middle even if you did get it out in one piece.

T: Good idea! What do you think is going to happen next? She's gone to bed. She's tired after all this hard work.

C: She might just give up.

T: She might.

C: What if someone takes the onion?

T: Who do you think might take it?

C: A burglar.

T: Let's turn the page and find out. When you read pages 4 and 5, think of this question: Why did Mrs. Brown wake up?

C: Ghost burglars.

T: Let's read to find out.

(All the children read.)

▼ pages 4–5

T: Why did Mrs. Brown wake up?

C: She thinks a burglar's in the house.

C: Not just thinks. There *are* burglars.

T: Those are both good points. Where did you get that idea from? What did you look at to find out that idea?

C: Because when it says, "The house was full of burglars."

T: That's right.

C: They look like ghosts.

T: Do you think she was scared?

C: No.

T: You don't? How do you know?

C: Because she's talking kind of quiet. She asks them if they want soup.

T: Good thinking.

C: *(Studying picture.)* She's trying to hide under the blanket.

T: Do you think she got scared when she woke up?

C: Yes.

T: But then she gets over that, because, as you say, she asks them if they want some soup.

C: The burglars might hate her and run away.

T: *(Addressing another child.)* What do you think?

C: Maybe she has a trap in the kitchen.

T: She may have.

C: Maybe she'll catch them in the pot!

▼ pages 6–8

T: That's an interesting idea! I never would have thought of that. Let's turn the page. Our next question is, How did Mrs. Brown get rid of the burglars? You'll find out if you read pages 6, 7, and 8 to the end of the story.

C: Will they steal things?

T: You read and find out and see if you're right.

C: I think they will.

T: Let's read and see. See if that's what the author said.

(All the children read.)

DISCUSSION

C: I think I know what they are—ghost burglars. Because one of them is slimy. *(Points to the picture.)* See, it looks slimy.

T: What else might that light spot be?

C: His eye.

C: On this page, they're crying droplets.

C: You feel like crying because onions get in your eyes and it stings.

C: I know. That happened to me when I made soup.

T: I see! Have you all read to the end of page 8?

All: Yes.

T: So, how did Mrs. Brown get rid of the burglars? What did she do?

C: She made them run away.

T: What did she do to make them run away?

C: She tricked them, because otherwise she wouldn't be smiling.

T: But how did she trick them? What didn't they like?

C: The onion soup. They tried to get away

from her horrible onion soup, because they thought it was horrible.

T: And why did they think it was horrible? What did it make them do?

C: Cry.

T: They cried and cried, didn't they? Do you think that was a good idea that she had?

All: Yes.

T: What were some of the big ideas, the main ideas in this story?

C: It was good thinking.

C: She might not have known they were burglars.

C: She might have just thought they were a lot of poor people.

T: Yes, she could have.

C: They probably thought she was rich because of the way she lived, because of the huge onion.

T: They might have. Has anything like this ever happened to you?

C: In my dreams.

MINI LANGUAGE LESSON

The teacher reviews the concept of similes and then asks the children to locate examples of similes in the story that describe how the burglars cried. As the children find the similes, the teacher writes them on a chart:

- The burglars cried like watering cans.
- The burglars cried like garden hoses.
- The burglars cried like floods and thunder storms.

The teacher then asks the children to make up some new similes to describe how the burglars cried and adds them to the list.

FOLLOW-UP ACTIVITY

T: Now I'd like you to think of what happened first in the story. We're going to make a time line of the story. Do you know what a time line is?

C: Yes, times of it [the story].

T: Yes. What happened first in the story?

C: She's trying to get her onion out to make onion soup.

T: Yes. *(Writes on board and reads aloud.)* One: Mrs. Brown was trying to get her onion out because she wanted to make onion soup. And then what happened next?

C: She cut the top off with her chain saw.

T: All right. *(Writes on board and reads aloud.)* Two: She cut the top off with her chain saw. What next?

C: The burglars came in.

T: What happened before the burglars came in?

C: She took all day to get it out.

T: Yes. So how did that make her feel?

C: Tired.

T: *(Writes on board and reads aloud.)* Three: She worked all day and got very tired, so she went to bed. What next?

C: The burglars came.

T: The burglars came. And then what happened? Because this is where she had a problem. There are burglars; they want her money. So what did she do?

C: She got her ax and cut the onion up—cut it all up and made them cry. Because the onion was horrible.

T: She tempted them with her soup, didn't she, because they were hungry for soup. So, she's making onion soup, and when she started cutting the onions, what happened to the burglars?

C: Started crying.

T: Can you find the place where it tells you what they do when she's cutting up the onion? It says that Mrs. Brown cried a little, and the burglars cried like...let's read it together. *(All the children read page 7.)*

T: What did the burglars cry like?

C: Garden hoses.

C: Because it [an onion] would do that to you, even twenty little onions.

A Guided Reading such as this can lead into a variety of follow-up activities. For example, the children could work in pairs or individually to finish creating time lines and illustrations showing the sequence of events in the story. They could write their thoughts about the story in individual literature response journals and/or share their thoughts in a group discussion.

You do not have to do an extensive follow-up activity with every book. Any follow-up activities should be meaningful and authentic and should relate naturally to the story. It is also effective to have children do paired reading at this time.

Guided Reading Format 2
Focus on beginning literature circles

Format 2 Outline
1. Story introduction
2. Silent reading
3. Discussion
4. Follow-up activity

1. Story introduction

(Each child has a copy of the book.)

▶ Involve the students in figuring out the title and discuss the cover illustrations.

▶ Provide a brief overview or main idea of the story.

2. Silent reading

▶ Students read the selection silently at their seats.

▶ Selection lengths may vary at this level from short stories to short chapter books.

▶ Students can react to their reading in a literature response journal.

3. Discussion

▶ Participate in beginning literature circles to discuss one or more of the literary elements found in the story.

▶ Share observations and opinions about the story.

▶ Share response journals.

4. Follow-up activity

▶ Have the children respond to or react to reading by using journals and/or literature-related activities or introduce a new story for the next day. The Guided Reading activity booklets contain ideas for follow-up activities relating to each book.

Strategy Prompts for the Early Fluency Level

Continue to focus on meaning, structure, and visual prompts from the upper emergent level.

Focus on self-correcting
- There is a difficult [or "tricky"] part here. Can you find it?
- Are you right? Could that be _____?
- Take a closer look at _____.
- How did you know that this word was _____?

Focus on cross-checking
- How did you know that was _____?
- Is there another way to tell?
- It could be _____, but look at _____.

Focus on self-monitoring
- Try that again.
- What did you notice?
- Were you right?
- How did you know?
- Why did you stop?

4

(This chart is the same as that given on page 39.)

FOCUS ON BEGINNING LITERATURE CIRCLES

Sloppy Tiger Bedtime by Joy Cowley (SUNSHINE Level 3)

Children at the early fluency level are ready to move on in Guided Reading sessions to begin involvement in *beginning literature circles*. In beginning literature circles, children read the story *prior* to meeting with the teacher for Guided Reading. The Guided Reading is followed by a circle discussion focusing on various literary concepts. Afterward, the children engage in mini language lessons before moving to a follow-up activity.

The following Guided Reading shows the process a teacher can use for beginning literature circles with early fluency students as they move toward fluency. The children read the story before meeting with the teacher. By doing this, they are challenged to read unfamiliar text independently. They then reread the story and work with language and literary concepts. They discuss the story in depth, attending to genre, characters, theme, vocabulary, and letter sounds, and conclude with a follow-up activity.

STORY INTRODUCTION AND SILENT READING

The teacher introduces the book and asks the children to read it silently prior to meeting in their Guided Reading group.

DISCUSSION

(Each child has a copy of the book.)

▼ **cover**

T: I see you have the book called *Sloppy Tiger Bedtime.* Did you read the story?

All: Yes!

T: Did you enjoy the story?

All: Yes!

C: No!

T: It wasn't one of your favorites, Sharon? Do you like the other Sloppy Tiger books?

C: Yes!

C: This is the same guy who did *Superkids* [SUNSHINE Level 1 Read-Togethers]. It says, Illustrations by Peter Stevenson.

T: Yes, he was the same illustrator for *Superkids.* That's exactly right. Now someone asked me what that thing on the cover is. Does anyone know what it is?

(The children shake their heads.)

T: It's a hot-water bottle. Why do you think he'd take a hot-water bottle to bed?

C: To keep warm.

T: That's right. People sometimes use a hot-water bottle to keep warm. Let's think about our story for just a moment. Was this a fiction or nonfiction story?

All: Fiction.

T: Fiction. Why was it a fiction story?

C: Because a girl can't have a tiger as a friend. Because if she has a tiger as a friend, that girl would be dead by now!

T: All right. Why else?

C: Because tigers eat people.

T: Because tigers might eat people. *(Addressing another child.)* Do you have a reason why it might be a fiction story?

C: Tigers don't sleep like that in a bed. They're really used to being outside, and if they're inside, they'll scratch everybody.

C: Tigers can't really play with toys.

T: Good thinking. Now, please put your books down in front of you. As you look at them, I want you to think about who the main characters were in the story. Who were the main characters?

C: A tiger.

T: A tiger. What kind of tiger?

C: Nice.

C: Sloppy Tiger.

T: Who can add to that? What else was he like?

C: Bad! Because when she wanted him to go to bed, he wouldn't go.

C: He was silly because he was scared about no stripes.

(More hands go up as the teacher continues to call on different children.)

C: He was so excited that he was going to hear a tiger story, he was biting his pillow.

(Laughter.)

C: He was a pain!

C: He was kind of sloppy when he brushed the bathroom.

T: Was there another important character?

C: The girl.

T: Yes, the girl is a main character, too. What was she like? Who can describe her?

C: She could act like a parent and was good at it.

C: She had curly hair.

C: Did she ever!

C: She was rude when she yelled at him.

C: When the tiger brushed the mirror when he was supposed to wash his teeth, she *yelled.*

T: What was she like?

C: She was a good reader.

C: In the beginning, she yelled at him to go brush. Then she turned nice at the end.

C: When she was mean, she looked like, "Don't mess with me!"

C: She got mad when he wouldn't go to bed.

T: Who can tell me what happened in the story?

C: The tiger didn't want to go to bed.

T: Raise your hand if you like to go to bed when it's time.

(No one raises a hand.)

T: None of you! Are you just like the Sloppy Tiger?

All: Yes!

T: What were some of the things the girl asked him to do before he went to bed?

C: Brush his teeth.

T: Did he brush his teeth right away?

C: No.

C: He watched TV.

T: He watched TV instead of brushing his teeth. Have you ever done that before?

All: Yes!

▼ **pages 2–3**

T: Let's turn in your books to page 2. What did the girl want the Sloppy Tiger to do?

C: Go to bed.

T: Go to bed. Did he do that?

All: No.

T: Can you find the sentence that tells that she really meant it when she told him to brush his teeth and go to bed? Put your fingers around that part. Where do you think it might be?

(The children find the sentence and frame it with their fingers.)

T: Maria? Can you read that for me?

C: *(Reading.)* He didn't answer...

T: Can you just find that one sentence that says that she really wants him to do that right now?

C: *(Reading.)* "Teeth and bed!" I told him. "At once!"

T: "At once!" And what's at the end of that sentence there?

C: Exclamation mark.

T: Do you think she really meant it?
All: Yes!
T: Yes!
C: She's saying, "Let's go! Brush those teeth and off to bed!"

▼ **pages 6–11**
T: Do you know anybody like the Sloppy Tiger?
C: My sister, definitely! She makes a big mess on the table at dinnertime.
T: What kind of mess?
C: She spills, and she eats with her hands.
C: My brother. He spills his milk and makes a big mess.
C: My brother spills his food and uses his hands, but it's better.
C: My friend Kelly is definitely a Sloppy Tiger. She growls when she bosses, and she bosses a lot.
C: My dog growls like a tiger.
T: What would you do to get Sloppy Tiger to go to bed on time?
C: Well, what I would do if he would not go to bed at the right time—I'd run and have him chase me, and then I'd run to his bed and he'd follow me, and then we'd get in his bed.
C: I'd get him his favorite bedtime thing. That would probably work.
C: I'd say, "You can't play tomorrow."
C: I would give him a present.
T: What kind of present?
C: It would be a toy. Then he'd go to bed.
C: I'd make him stay up until he got bored. I'd keep saying, "You have to stay up," until he begged me to go to bed. Then I'd put him to bed.
C: I'd get him ice cream and when he reached for it, I'd say, "Not until you get in bed!"

MINI LANGUAGE LESSONS

Notice that here the teacher incorporates several mini language lessons in the discussion of this book. The children identify the contraction *didn't*, identify the *st* letter combination in the word *story*, list other words that begin or end with *st*, and discuss the meaning of the word *pretend*.

▼ **pages 4–5**
T: Let's turn to page 4. There's a contraction on this page. Who can find that contraction? *(The children search for the contraction* didn't *and frame it with their fingers.)*

T: I see some of you have found it. What I need you to do is to tell me what contraction it is.

C: *Didn't.*

T: *Didn't.* And *didn't* means the same as...

C: Did not.

T: Very good! Let's read that sentence together.

T&C: *(Reading.)* But he didn't want to go to bed.

T: Look at page 5.

C: He's *really* made a mess.

C: Soap in her hair!

▼ pages 10–11

T: Let's turn to page 10 now. I'd like you to tell me what kind of story the tiger wanted to hear. What kind of story did Sloppy Tiger want for a bedtime story?

C: Sloppy Tiger.

C: He wanted a story about tigers.

T: Can you find the sentence that tells me what kind of story he wanted? Ben?

C: *(Reading.)* He wanted a story about tigers.

T: Yes. We found that he wanted a story about tigers. Now I want you to look at that word *story.* What sound does that *s-t* make? *(Encouraging the children to use their sense of oral language.)*

All: *(Making sound of letter combination.)* S-s-s-t.

T: Let's all say it.

T&C: S-s-s-t.

T: Can you think of a word that has the *st* sound at the beginning?

C: *Static.*

T: Great! *Static.*

C: Stand.

T: *Stand!* Good work.

C: Stocking.

T: *Stocking,* yes.

C: Steak.

T: Good work! Now, let's get a little tricky. Can you—

C: *Stork!*

T: Yes, *stork* is another *st* word. Good job. Now, can you think of a word that has the *st* at the end?

(Silence as the children think.)

T: What grade are we in?

All: First!

T: What do you hear at the end?

C: *St!*

C: *Mast.*

T: A *mast.* Good job. Let's turn to page—

C: *Must.*

T: *Must.* Good one!

▼ pages 14–15

T: On page 14, can you find the word that means make-believe? What is it?

C: *Pretend.*

T: *Pretend.* Have you ever pretended something?

C: I pretended to have lemonade on me.

C: I pretended to go to sleep.

T: You pretended to go to sleep! How?

C: When my mom tells me to go to bed, I go like this *(folding arms under head and closing eyes)* and snore.

(The teacher and children laugh.)

T: OK! I'm glad you enjoyed that story. What I need you to do is to take a new Sloppy Tiger book home and read it to your mom or dad tonight. That new book is *Sloppy Tiger and the Party* [SUNSHINE Level 3]. We'll talk about it tomorrow.

FOLLOW-UP ACTIVITY

The next day, the class discusses *Sloppy Tiger and the Party* by Joy Cowley and its story structure. Then they compare the story structure of *Sloppy Tiger Bedtime* with *Sloppy Tiger and the Party* by listing the ways the stories are alike and different.

Remember that you do not have to do an extensive follow-up activity with every book. Any follow-up activities should be meaningful and authentic and should relate naturally to the story.

Summary

The Guided Reading formats and models in this manual are meant only as guidelines for you to follow as you integrate Guided Reading in your classroom. Sometimes you will combine two steps of the format or eliminate a step you decide is not needed with a particular group. As you become more experienced with Guided Reading, your use of the progressive formats will become more fluid and natural. Just as the children in your classroom gradually move toward fluency in their reading through practice, you will move toward effective use of Guided Reading as part of your reading program.

Chapter 5
Using Nonfiction in Guided Reading

Nonfiction and Young Readers

In both fiction and nonfiction, we can learn about people, animals, science, history, and the world around us. Often fiction and nonfiction become blended together within the same book. The book may appear to be part of a fantasy or fiction genre, and yet it will be interspersed with a great deal of factual information.

Children are drawn to nonfiction as they encounter and explore the world. They naturally want to learn more about their world, and nonfiction books often hold the answers that propel young readers in new directions of inquiry.

Nonfiction promotes the discovery of how facts are presented and the relationship of concepts or information to our lives and our world. The overall purpose of nonfiction is to gain knowledge and understanding from what was read and to inspire the reader to want to know more.

Nonfiction Classifications

Nonfiction books can be divided into several classifications or genres. Several basic categories of nonfiction books are defined here. Some nonfiction books will incorporate elements of more than one format.

REPORTING FORMAT

Reporting format books use a basic reporting style to organize, document, or present information from any of the content areas, such as social studies, science, or health. An example of a reporting format is *The Hermit Crab* by Brian and Jillian Cutting (SUNSHINE Level 1 Fact and Fantasy). This book gives the reader descriptive information about the hermit crab.

PROCEDURAL FORMAT

Procedural books tell the reader how to do something or how to make something. Through their reading, students might learn how to set up a science experiment, how to follow directions in a recipe, or how to create an art project. Procedural books usually involve a step-by-step process. *Our Tree House* by Rebel Williams (TWiG® Read-Togethers) gives the reader an idea of how to build a tree house, from drawing up the plans to having a party in the completed tree house.

EXPLANATION FORMAT

Explanation books show or tell the reader how things work or why things happen and often use a sequential or cause-and-effect pattern to express the ideas. *Rain or Shine?* by Rebel Williams (TWiG Emergent Readers, Set E) explains why whimsical proverbs can be used to forecast the weather. Cause and effect are used throughout the book to show how an event in nature explains and affects the weather.

RECOUNTING FORMAT

Recounting books reconstruct an event in a logical sequence that leads to the conclusion. These books describe what has happened, are often written in the past tense, and may be in the form of a narrative. *Good-bye, Perky* by Miriam Frost (TWiG Emergent Readers, Set F) tells about the death of a pet bird and its burial.

PERSUASIVE FORMAT

Persuasive books are those that try to convince the reader to accept a point of view or to take a position on an issue. They often give reasons and recommendations to support a position or issue. A typical example of persuasive text is an advertisement. An example of a persuasive format book is *The Park Street Playground* by Joy Cowley (SUNSHINE Safety Books). In this story, the children try to convince the mayor that they need a new playground and then have to persuade their parents to help them fix the old playground.

NARRATIVE INFORMATION FORMAT

Narrative information books inform the reader by providing factual information in a narrative structure through the use of characters, settings, and other literary devices. Narratives can convey the necessary information to the reader and often help make the facts more memorable and more easily understood.

An example of a narrative information book is *It's Not the Same* by Judy Gilbert and Adele Graham (SUNSHINE Level 3 Fact and Fantasy). The little girl in this book tells her story of changing schools and how she learns to accept her new school. This story lends itself easily to a comparative study of her old school and the new one. With informational books, comparisons are frequently used to explain concepts, ideas, and factual information.

Nonfiction and Thinking Processes

Nonfiction can play a key role in early literacy; it connects children with expository writing and requires that they use thinking processes different from those used for reading fiction. When using nonfiction with Guided Reading groups, the children should begin noticing the important and specific details typically found in this category of writing. Nonfiction materials will require students to use some of the following thinking processes:

- Reading for information
- Understanding and creating diagrams and charts
- Understanding cause and effect
- Finding and understanding the problem and solution
- Comparing two or more concepts or ideas
- Sequencing information
- Identifying the characteristics of something
- Determining the historical significance of events or people
- Differentiating between fact and fiction or fact and opinion
- Recognizing propaganda
- Summarizing and generalizing from information
- Drawing conclusions
- Making predictions and assumptions
- Documenting data or information
- Evaluating what was read
- Determining the relevancy of material read

5

Nonfiction in Guided Reading

Using nonfiction in Guided Reading groups is like using fiction for Guided Reading. Nonfiction books at the early emergent, upper emergent, and early fluency levels should provide the same support system as Guided Reading fiction books. They need to be predictable; use natural language; contain rhyme, rhythm, and repetition; and have illustrations that closely match the text.

The process for using nonfiction books in a Guided Reading session with early emergent, upper emergent, and early fluency levels is the same as the process for using fiction for Guided Reading. Multiple copies of each nonfiction book are needed so that each child can have his or her own copy of the book to read. The only difference in the Guided Reading process may be in some of the teacher's questioning strategies. The teacher will need to ask probing questions and ask for predictions that will help students discover answers or arouse their curiosity.

Nonfiction Guided Reading Lessons (Early Emergent Level)

Early emergent readers are those students just learning that illustrations and books can tell a story, stimulate curiosity, or provide answers.

Nonfiction books at the early emergent level have many of the same characteristics found in fiction books at this level. Some nonfiction series from The Wright Group that are appropriate for early emergent readers include TWiG Emergent Readers, Sets A–D, and Wonder World.

BUG-WATCHING BY REBEL WILLIAMS (TWIG EMERGENT READERS, SET B)

You may want to review the Guided Reading format for the early emergent level on pages 14–15 before going on to the Guided Reading lesson below. One way to begin the Guided Reading time is by asking questions that focus on the nonfiction elements of the book. Some possible questions are

- What do you see on the cover of this story?
- Can you tell what the children might be doing by what they have in their hands?
- What are they holding?
- What could they use the flashlight and magnifying glass for?
- What do you know about bugs?
- Where can you find bugs?

Continue reading through the book following the early emergent process for Guided Reading. Have the students predict and confirm what they find out about bugs and their habitats.

You might want to discuss the safety factor in this book, showing that the boy and girl never touched or disturbed any of the bugs but only observed them. The last page of the story promotes curiosity and encourages students to research and discover the answers.

Children could then work independently or in pairs on related activities, such as researching the bugs in the book, keeping an OIR (observe/illustrate/record) journal on insect collections in the classroom, or making a feature analysis matrix. The feature analysis matrix could include the name of the bug, where it lives, and its color, habitat, and so on.

EVERY MORNING BY REBEL WILLIAMS (TWIG EMERGENT READERS, SET C)

Another example of Guided Reading at the early emergent level uses the book *Every Morning*. Begin the Guided Reading by focusing on questions that deal with nonfiction elements. Some possible questions are

- What do you think this book might be about?
- What time of day is it on the cover?
- What do you do every morning when you wake up?
- How do you feel or act in the morning?

Continue reading the book using the early emergent process for Guided Reading. Have students predict and confirm their ideas of what happens every morning in the story. The last page of this book sparks students' curiosity about animals that go to sleep in the morning.

The children could then work independently or in pairs to find out what animals are awake at night. They could then compare and contrast those animals with ones that are awake in the daytime.

Another activity might be to find other animals that start with a different letter, such as *d* for dog, deer, duck, dolphin, and so on to make a new *Every Morning* book. Children could also make a chart or time line that shows what time they get up, eat, brush their teeth, and so on.

Nonfiction Guided Reading Lessons (Upper Emergent Level)

Children reading at the upper emergent level already grasp many of the basic concepts of print and are ready for more complex books. These students are developing independence by beginning to integrate strategies and are gaining more meaning from print.

Some nonfiction series from The Wright Group that are appropriate for upper emergent readers include TWiG Emergent Readers, Sets E–F; TWiG Read-Togethers; SUNSHINE Level 1 Fact and Fantasy; SUNSHINE Science, Level 1; and Wonder World.

MACHINES BY FRED AND JEANNE BIDDULPH (SUNSHINE SCIENCE, LEVEL 1, SET C)

You may want to review the Guided Reading formats for the upper emergent level on pages 24–25 and 30–31 before going on to the Guided Reading lesson below. One way to begin the Guided Reading time is by asking questions that focus on the nonfiction elements of the book. Some possible questions are

- What do you know about machines?
- What do machines do?
- What is the purpose of machines?
- What machines do you use every day?

Go through the book following the upper emergent process for Guided Reading. Have the students predict and confirm what they found out about machines and their uses. You might want to discuss how all of the machines in this book can be classified as simple machines. The last page in the book provides a summary statement that lends itself to students creating their own summaries or generalizations about machines.

Students could then work independently or in pairs to find out more about simple machines, to create a feature analysis matrix that shows all of the characteristics for each simple machine, to make a list of all the machines found in the classroom or that they use at home, or to compare and contrast how to do a particular job with and without a machine. For example, have students compare sharpening a pencil without using a pencil sharpener of any kind with using a handheld pencil sharpener, a wall pencil sharpener, and an electric pencil sharpener. They could then summarize what makes using a machine easier.

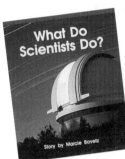

WHAT DO SCIENTISTS DO? BY MARCIE BOVETZ (TWIG EMERGENT READERS, SET E)

Another example for teaching Guided Reading at the upper emergent level is the book *What Do Scientists Do?* Begin the Guided Reading by asking questions that focus on the informational aspect of the book. Some possible questions are

- What do you see in the picture on the cover?
- What do you think scientists do?
- What are some different things scientists study?
- What scientific tools or instruments might scientists need to study something?

Continue reading the book using the upper emergent process for Guided Reading. Have students predict and confirm the different areas for scientific study. The last page of the book encourages readers to think about something that they would like to study. The students could then begin gathering materials that they might need for their own scientific research. They might also use an OIR (observe/illustrate/record) activity for their chosen area.

In pairs or small groups, children could research the names for scientists who study

5

specific areas using the following pattern:

> **A scientist who studies _____**
> **is a/an _____.**

The children could also draw and label the different tools or instruments a scientist might use, such as a microscope to study germs or a satellite map to study the weather.

Nonfiction Guided Reading Lessons (Early Fluency Level)

Students at the early fluency level are beginning to achieve independence by integrating meaning, structure, and varied text. Books at this level still continue to provide some repetitive text and to build on vocabulary already introduced. Early fluency readers are still developing an understanding of literary elements.

Some series from The Wright Group that are appropriate for early fluency readers include SUNSHINE Levels 2–5 Fact and Fantasy and SUNSHINE Science, Level 2.

TRACKS IN THE SAND BY ANN GOODALE (SUNSHINE LEVEL 2 FACT AND FANTASY)

You may want to review the Guided Reading formats for the early fluency level on pages 38–39 and 43 before going on to the Guided Reading lesson below. One way to begin the Guided Reading session is by asking questions that focus on nonfiction elements of the book. Some possible questions are

- Have you ever been to a sandy area and either seen tracks or made tracks?

- How can you tell what animals made the tracks in the sand?

- What do you know about an animal by looking at its tracks?

Continue through the story following the early fluency process for Guided Reading. Have the students predict and confirm what they found out about animal tracks. You may want to discuss characteristics of animal tracks following the reading.

Pages 22 and 23 of *Tracks in the Sand* provide an opportunity for children to put their knowledge of animal tracks to use by matching the various tracks to the appropriate animal. The last page of the book encourages creativity by asking the children to make their own mystery tracks.

Children could then work independently or in pairs to research other animal tracks and their characteristics, to compare and contrast different tracks, or to create diagrams or illustrations of a single animal and its tracks.

WONDERFUL EARS BY BRIAN AND JILLIAN CUTTING (SUNSHINE SCIENCE, LEVEL 2, SET B)

This book provides another example for Guided Reading at the early fluency level. Begin the Guided Reading by asking questions that focus on the informational aspects of the book. Some possible questions are

- What do you think this book might be about?

- What do we know about ears?

- What information would you like to know about ears?

- How do you think the ears of other animals might differ from ours? How are they the same as ours?

Read the book following the early fluency process for Guided Reading. This book uses a question-and-answer format that encourages students to predict and then read to confirm their predictions. *Wonderful Ears* also uses charts, diagrams, illustrations, and photos to relate its message.

Related activities for this book might include making a feature analysis matrix that compares characteristics of animal ears, making diagrams of different kinds of ears, or doing experiments to see how well our ears hear sounds in various circumstances.

Graphic Organizers

Follow-up discussions for nonfiction Guided Reading groups should focus on concepts and content. Graphic organizers are useful ways to facilitate these discussions by providing a visual representation of the information acquired. Their varied formats allow children to verbally and visually summarize and depict this new information. Graphic organizers are designed to motivate children, actively involve them, and help them organize information.

To facilitate understanding, children might engage in any of the following graphic organizer activities:

- KWL chart: records what students *know* about a topic, what they *want* to learn, and later what they have *learned* about that topic.

- Feature analysis matrix: compares and contrasts various characteristics of a topic or concept.

- Graphs, charts, diagrams: visually record or show information.

- OIR (observe/illustrate/record): children observe something (with their eyes, a microscope, a magnifying glass, or in any other visual way), draw what they observe, and then write about (record) that observation.

- Venn diagram: shows similarities and differences between two or more objects, concepts, or ideas.

- Journals: record information, thoughts, and ideas.

- Sequence charts and time lines: show a sequence of events or the chronological order of events.

- Essays, reports, research papers: record information in a presentation format.

- Information webs: organize and sort information into different categories.

- Problem/solutions/effects matrix (or problem/effects/solution matrix): shows a problem being

addressed, the solution or possible solutions, and what effects the problem and/or solutions have on people, animals, and the environment.

- Art projects: personalize the learning experience.

With any of the graphic organizers mentioned here, it is always a good idea to encourage children to write a summary of what they have learned from the organizational process. When children are able to generalize or summarize what they have learned, they are using higher-level thinking strategies and become much more capable of being able to make what they have learned their own.

Several types of graphic organizers are shown in chart 4, "Types of Charted Discussions."

Chart 4

Types of Charted Discussions

Comparisons

Alligator	Crocodile
Summary:	

Fact and Fiction

Real	Make-Believe
Summary:	

Cause and Effect

Condition	Effect on growth
Soil	
Sand	
Fertilizer	
No sun	
Sun	
Summary:	

Relationships

Animal	Environment
Summary:	

Problems, Solutions, and Effects

Problem	Solutions	Good for animals	Good for people	Good for the environment
You find a spider in the shower.				
Summary statement:				

5

Summary

Nonfiction and informational books help provide experiences and environments that facilitate the learning process. When students are immersed in reading books from all genres, they grow in their understanding of the world, of themselves, and as readers.

The goal of using nonfiction in the daily Guided Reading program is to spark children's curiosity in the world around them and to provide opportunities for children to explore and discover that world as independent thinkers and learners.

Chapter 6

Evaluation of Reading

Record-Keeping Strategies

Described below are several ways to keep track of a student's reading development. Combine them with record-keeping strategies that have worked well in your classroom.

Reading Folder (Literary Record)

An individual reading folder for each child provides a ready reference to the child's reading development. The reading folder contains all the other record-keeping materials described below: the individual student reading log, the poetry and song menu, and any anecdotal records. It is also the place to keep a record of the child's favorite literature (books, poems, and songs) and reading-record evaluations, which are explained later in this section. Include a writing sample, if you wish.

Individual Student Reading Log

A reading log is simply a checklist for keeping track of which books a student has read. Your students should be encouraged to read freely, ranging from level to level and book to book according to their interests and developmental levels.

Poetry and Song Menu

A poetry and song menu is a list of the songs and poems that a child learns by heart throughout the year. A parent can use the menu to select a poem or song that he or she would like to hear. On your menu, you may wish to type in the names of all the poems and songs you intend to use throughout the year and then photocopy that list for each child. You or the child then puts a star next to each poem or song that is learned by heart. You might also choose to write in only the poems and songs that each child learns. Suggest to the children that they make "a gift of a poem" on special occasions, reciting a poem they have learned to a friend or family member on a holiday or birthday.

Anecdotal Records

Anecdotal records can include almost anything children say and do: contributions and behavior during Shared Reading, interaction with other children, behavior when working independently, statements, jokes, and any other instances that capture a child's personality. Taken as a whole, these "slice of life" observations form a picture of a child that complements other records and

more formal observations. Some teachers write anecdotes on adhesive address labels or gummed pieces of paper and then stick these on paper in the child's folder. Parents will especially enjoy these records.

Assessment Tools

Evaluating a child's reading on a regular basis in the context of an actual reading session provides a systematic record of the child's development. In addition, you have an "instant" analysis that allows you to tailor your teaching strategies to meet that child's needs in a timely fashion.

In this section, we explain the use of several important tools for teachers of early emergent, upper emergent, and early fluency level readers: the Concepts of Print Checklists for the emergent level and for the early fluency level, the Concepts of Literature Checklist for the early fluency level, and the reading record. We also discuss teaching strategies you can use once you've gleaned information from your evaluations of students.

If you wish to know more about evaluation, read the following, all by Mary M. Clay: *The Early Detection of Reading Difficulties* (Heinemann 1985); *Reading Recovery: A Guidebook for Teachers in Training* (Heinemann 1993); or *An Observation Survey of Early Literacy Achievement* (Heinemann 1993). Marie Clay is considered a pioneer in the field. She is most noted for the development of the Reading Recovery Program, which originated in New Zealand and is now in use throughout the United States. Her diagnostic survey was originally developed to identify those children who might need more direct help through the Reading Recovery Program in acquiring effective reading behaviors and strategies. Her work provides in-depth information on evaluations and the conventions used in taking a reading record.

Concepts of Print Checklists (Emergent Levels)

In this section, we discuss the Concepts of Print Checklists for the emergent levels (early emergent and upper emergent). There are two checklists: one for evaluation of individuals and one for evaluation of groups. (Both are shown

Concepts of Print Checklist (Emergent Levels): Individual Profile

Name: _____ Date: _____

Teacher Questions	+	✔	−	Concept
Before reading, ask the child:				
Where is the front of the book?				Book concepts—front cover
Where is the back of the book?				Book concepts—back cover
Can you point to the title?				Book concepts—title
Can you point to the title page?				Book concepts—title page
Which page do we read first?				Directionality—beginning of text
Where does it tell the story?				Reading concepts—print carries the message
Which way do we go when we're reading?				Directionality—left-to-right in a sentence
Where do we go when we get to the end of the line?				Directionality—return sweep
During reading, ask yourself:				
As the child reads and points to the text, is there an exact match between number of words spoken and number of words printed?				Reading concepts—one-to-one correspondence
After reading, ask the child:				
Can you put your fingers around a word?				Word concept
Can you find two words that are the same?				Word concept
Where is the first word on this page?				First word
Where is the last word on this page?				Last word
Can you put your fingers around a letter?				Letter concept
Can you tell me the names of some letters on the page?				Letter concept
Can you find a capital letter?				Capital letter
Can you find a small letter?				Small letter
What's this? . (period)				Punctuation marks
, (comma)				
? (question mark)				
" " (quotation marks)				

Notes:

here in reduced form. Full-size checklists for photocopying can be found on pages 75–76.)

The Concepts of Print Checklist (Emergent Levels): Individual Profile shown here is designed to aid in evaluating a child's understanding of the basic concepts of print, an understanding that is essential to experiencing success early on in reading. Listed in this checklist are questions that focus on key abilities. The checklist is used with any book in a one-on-one session with a child.

The Concepts of Print Checklist is actually more than a tool for assessing a child's understanding of the concepts of print. It is also designed to familiarize the teacher with these concepts and with what he or she should be looking for when observing a child.

Eventually, as with other evaluation techniques, you will "absorb" the process and begin to spot details of the child's behavior without referring to the checklist at every turn. For example, if a child opens a book and begins reading the first sentence starting on the left-hand side, it will be clear to you that the child understands directionality and basic "book concepts."

Note that you do not need to check every item on the list each time a child reads to you. Your focus may change from one session to the next, much as you would change the topic of your mini language lessons. Above all, remember that a reading done for evaluation should still be conducted in an informal atmosphere. It is important for the child to feel that you are both enjoying the reading, not that he or she is being tested or grilled.

Concepts of Print Checklist (Emergent Levels): Class Profile

Date: _____

Student Names

Directionality (demonstrates)
- Left-to-right page sequence
- Left-to-right in sentence
- Return sweep
- Reading top to bottom
- Starting at beginning of book
- Finishing at end of book

Reading Concepts (points to)
- Text (print tells the story)
- Each word (one-to-one correspondence)

Book Concepts (can identify)
- Cover of book
- Title
- Title page

Words/Letters (can identify)
- A letter
- A word
- The first word on a page
- The last word on a page
- A first letter
- A last letter
- A capital letter
- A small letter
- Names of some letters
- Key words in isolation

Punctuation (can identify)
- Question mark (?)
- Period (.)
- Comma (,)
- Quotation marks (" ")

Strategies Used
- Relies on memory for reading
- Uses pictures to tell story in own words
- Uses pictures to help with words
- Uses language patterns
- Uses structure knowledge
- Uses beginning letter sounds
- Uses many letter sounds
- Uses background experience

Begin by recording the child's name and the date. Then give the child a book and begin asking the questions listed in the first section of the checklist (the "before reading" questions). These questions focus on basic book and reading concepts and on directionality.

Evaluate the child's response and mark one of the three middle columns for each question. Mark the "+" column if the child has clearly mastered the concept. Mark the "–" column if the child clearly does not understand the concept. Mark the "√" column if the child grasps the concept to a certain degree but does not fully comprehend it. You would mark this middle column if, for example, the child hesitates before answering correctly or answers incorrectly and then self-corrects.

6

The second section of the checklist asks you, the teacher, an important question to guide you in your evaluation: "As the child reads and points to the text, is there an exact match between number of words spoken and number of words printed?" In other words, is the child exhibiting one-to-one correspondence between spoken and written words? The action of reading aloud and pointing to each word is necessary in order to evaluate this concept. Again, mark one of the middle columns to reflect the child's skill level.

After the child has finished reading, conclude by asking the "after reading" questions in the third section of the checklist. These questions are pointed inquiries about specific concepts of print regarding letters, words, and punctuation. Record your evaluation. Any ideas or concerns you may have at the moment can be jotted in the "Notes" section at the bottom of the checklist.

Although evaluation of children's understanding of concepts of print is done throughout the school day both formally and informally, you may wish to focus on these concepts during Guided Reading. If you wish to use a form to evaluate a group, use the Concepts of Print Checklist (Emergent Levels): Class Profile.

Guided Reading Quick Evaluation Sheet

Another evaluation form to use with a group is the Guided Reading Quick Evaluation Sheet. With this simple form, you can record a few concepts or skills you wish to evaluate with a Guided Reading group. A sample filled-out form is shown

here. (A full-size sheet for photocopying can be found on page 77.) The Guided Reading Quick Evaluation Sheet can be used with Guided Reading groups at any reading level.

Concepts of Print Checklist (Early Fluency Level)

The Concepts of Print Checklist (Early Fluency Level) shown here focuses on more sophisticated concepts of print than those evaluated at the emergent levels. Listed on the early fluency checklist are points to evaluate in the areas of semantics (meaning), syntax (grammar), graphophonics (sounds and symbols), punctuation, and language strategies. The checklist may be used with any book in a one-on-one session with a child or with a Guided Reading group. (A full-size two-page

Guided Reading Quick Evaluation Sheet

Skills	Ivy	Jamal	Susan	Charles	Midori		
One-to-one correspondence	−	+	+	−	✓		
Return Sweep	✓	✓	+	✓	+		
Title	✓	+	+	✓	+		
Finding a word	−	+	✓	✓	✓		

Notes Jamal and Midori and Susan are wonderful models for the group. Midori has been progressing quickly - she can now isolate a word when asked to find one on the page (instead of framing sentences!). All students are confidently using return sweep. Ivy and Charles hesitated when asked to find the title — but they found it, then confirmed by watching others. Both Ivy and Charles need more guided practice on their one-to-one correspondence; need to make them aware of strategies for self-correction. Midori is self-correcting regularly now.

58

Concepts of Print Checklist (Early Fluency Level)

Date: _____

Names

Semantics *(meaning)*
Can identify:
- Opposites
- Compound words
- Homophones
- Synonyms
- Vocabulary
- Main idea
- Words in languages other than English
- Idioms

Syntax *(grammar)*
Can identify in books and use in writing:
- Naming words (nouns)
- Proper nouns
- Action words (verbs)
- Linking words (conjunctions)
- Describing words (adjectives and adverbs)
- Prepositions (location words)
- Plurals
- Pronouns
- Word endings and their purposes
- Simple sentences
- Paragraphs

Graphophonics *(sounds and symbols)*
Can identify in books and use in writing:
- Initial and final consonants and their sounds
- Letter combinations and their sounds
- Short vowel sounds
- Long vowel sounds
- Word families and their sounds
- Rhyming words

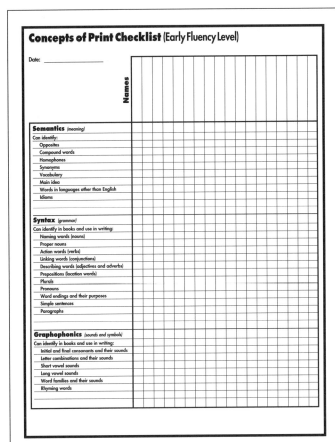

Concepts of Print Checklist (Early Fluency Level) continued

Date: _____

Names

Punctuation
Can identify and give purpose of:
- Period (.)
- Question mark (?)
- Exclamation point (!)
- Quotation marks (" ")
- Comma (,)
- Apostrophe (')
- Ellipses (…)
- Dash (—)
- Unusual typeface (bold, italic, etc.)

Language Strategies
Uses semantic cue system:
- Story sense
- Logic
- Background experience
- Pictorial and graphic resources

Uses syntactic cue system:
- Structure knowledge
- Language patterns
- Word endings

Uses graphophonic cue system:
- Beginning sounds
- Ending sounds
- Medial sounds
- Letter combinations
- Short and long vowel sounds
- Rhyming sounds

Cross-checks (makes predictions using more than one cue system)

---

checklist for photocopying can be found on pages 78–79.) If you wish to evaluate only a few skills or strategies, you may choose to use the Guided Reading Quick Evaluation Sheet discussed previously.

Concepts of Literature Checklist (Early Fluency Level)

The Concepts of Literature Checklist (Early Fluency Level) includes items to evaluate in the areas of story structure, literary terms, literary devices, and literary strategies (a full-size checklist for photocopying can be found on page 80):

- Story structure includes characterization, climax, sequence of events (plot), and type of story.

- Literary terms include character, setting, problem and solution, dialogue, and genre.

- Literary devices include similes, exaggeration, and word play.

Concepts of Literature Checklist (Early Fluency Level)

Date: _____

Names

Story Structure (can identify)
- Beginning, middle, and end
- Characterization
- Story climax
- Sequence of events

Literary Terms (can identify)
- Character
- Hero/villain
- Setting
- Problem
- Solution
- Point of view
- Dialogue
- Author/illustrator
- Stage directions
- Genre: Fiction
  - Nonfiction
  - Diary/journal
  - Biography
  - Drama/play
  - Poetry

Literary Devices (can identify)
- Similes
- Metaphors
- Alliteration
- Onomatopoeia
- Exaggeration
- Word play

Literary Strategies
- Uses table of contents
- Skims for facts
- Uses dictionary/encyclopedia
- Summarizes
- Retells
- Compares and contrasts
- Questions

6

- The literary strategies section allows you to evaluate particular strategies that the children are able to use successfully, such as using reference materials, summarizing, and making comparisons.

Reading Record

A reading record is more complex than an evaluation using the Concepts of Print Checklist or the Concepts of Literature Checklist. Evaluation using a reading record is done to analyze a child's use of reading strategies. Such an evaluation provides a more in-depth assessment of reading development.

A reading record is the same type of evaluation indicated by the terms "running record" or "miscue analysis." The latter is often used by reading specialists and can be very complicated. The reading record explained on these pages is a compact, more accessible version of miscue analysis that lends itself to general use in the average classroom.

As you take reading records, you'll find that this method becomes an unconscious part of your ability to observe reading strategies employed by your students. It is as much a development tool for you as it is an assessment tool for your class. You might take five or six reading records before you begin to feel comfortable and at ease with the process.

Taking a reading record is a five-step process that involves the use of a reading-record form, special notations as the child reads, and a few simple formulas. Each step of the following process is explained in depth in this section:

1. Reading and record-taking (listening to a child read and recording his or her reading behaviors)
2. Retelling (listening to a child retell a story to see if he or she understood it)
3. Calculating error, accuracy, and self-correction rates
4. Analyzing reading by using a reading record
5. Identifying appropriate teaching strategies

Chart 5

Reading Behavior Notations

Behavior Example		Notation
1. Substitution	horse / zebra	"Run!" said the horse / zebra.
2. Omission of a word	(some)	In go (some) socks.
3. Insertion of a word	big ∧	I love my big ∧ sister.
4. Using letter cues	m___ / monkey	The m___ monkey tells the tiger.
5. Repetition of word or phrase	I gobble ⌐R	I gobble ⌐R up dragons.
6. Self-correction	busy s/c / buzzing	They are buzzing busy s/c around the ham.

READING AND RECORD-TAKING

In the first step, you record a child's reading behavior as he or she reads. You are an observer and do not offer any directions or prompting. The purpose of the reading record determines which text you select. For example, to determine if the child is ready to progress to more complex texts, provide a book at the child's current reading level that the child has not yet read (taking care not to use a book that could elicit too high a level of frustration). But to just see how well the child is reading at his or her current level, use a familiar book at that level or one that was recently presented.

As the child reads, you will want to be aware of the following six reading behaviors as you take notes:

- **Substitution:** substituting an incorrect word or phrase for the correct word or phrase

- **Omission:** omitting a word, a part of a word, or a phrase

- **Insertion:** inserting a word, a part of a word, or a phrase

- **Using letter cues:** attempting to decode a word by sounding it out letter by letter (or syllable by syllable)

- **Repetition:** repeating a word or a phrase

- **Self-correction:** correcting an incorrectly read or omitted word or phrase by going back and rereading

You'll need a copy of the text from the chosen book in order to mark it with the symbols shown in chart 5, "Reading Behavior Notations." Prepare this copy by photocopying the text or by typing or writing it out clearly. (If you do not wish to reproduce the text for marking, you can simply make check marks on the chart to indicate correctly read words and use the notation symbols to indicate when the child being evaluated uses letter cues to sound out a word or to identify particular words that pose problems.)

The notation symbols refer to the six reading behaviors listed in chart 5. You make these notations on your copy of the text as the child reads aloud. The first column in the chart lists the behaviors, the second shows which notation is used to record each behavior, and the third shows how your text will look when marked with notations.

Chart 6, "Sample Reading Record," diagrams a reading record using the book *Along Comes Jake* by Joy Cowley (SUNSHINE Level 1, Set F). The actual text of the book is contained in the first column. The next column shows how the child read it. The third column represents the teacher's copy of the text, marked with notations recording the child's reading of the story. The fourth column specifies the relevant reading behaviors exhibited by the child.

A tape recorder is an invaluable aid in your early efforts at taking reading records. Recording the child allows you to listen to the tape at a later time and make your notations then. You'll be able to stop and start the recording, which will give you time to make the proper notations and to familiarize yourself with the process. You won't have to worry about missing something (especially with fast readers!).

Chart 6

Sample Reading Record:
Along Comes Jake (SUNSHINE Level 1, Set F)

Actual Text	Text as Child Read It	Text with Teacher's Reading Record Notations	Reading Behaviors
Ben helps Anne with the bed.	Ben helps Anne make the bed.	Ben helps Anne ~~with~~ the bed. *(make)*	Substitution
Anne helps Dad with the garden.	Anne helps Dad make the garden.	Anne helps Dad ~~with~~ the garden. *(make)*	Substitution
Ben helps Mom with the painting.	Ben helps m-...Mom with the f-...paint...painting.	Ben helps Mom with the painting. *(m— f-/paint/s/c)*	Using letter cues Self-correction
And then along comes Jake!	And along comes Jake!	And (then) along comes Jake!	Omission
Mom helps Dad with the car.	Mom helps Dad make the car.	Mom helps Dad ~~with~~ the car. *(make)*	Substitution
Dad helps Ben with the washing.	Dad helps Ben with the washing.	Dad helps Ben with the washing.	Correct reading
Anne helps Mom with the bathroom.	Anne helps Mom with the b-...clean.	Anne helps Mom with the ~~bathroom~~. *(b—/clean)*	Substitution
And then along comes Jake!	And along comes Jake!	And (then) along comes Jake!	Omission
Ben helps Dad with the windows.	Ben helps Dad with the windows.	Ben helps Dad with the windows.	Correct reading
Dad helps Mom with the wood.	Dad helps Mom with the wood.	Dad helps Mom with the wood.	
Mom helps Ben with the bike.	Mom helps Ben with the bike.	Mom helps Ben with the bike.	

Most important, the tape recorder frees you to observe the child closely and note other important reading behaviors, such as using picture clues to make predictions and reacting to unfamiliar words by either scanning the text or fixating on the word alone. With practice, however, you will soon develop your recording skills until you can make notations automatically when you observe a reading behavior.

RETELLING

Having the child retell the story he or she has just read reveals the child's comprehension of meaning. The retelling should be informal; it is not meant to be a word-for-word replay. Don't ask the child to tell you the story; ask him or her to tell you *about* the story. For example, ask the child, "Tell me about the story, just like you would tell it to a friend who hasn't heard it." Then listen carefully to discern how well the

child understood the story's meaning. Note, too, how well the child recalls who the characters are and what the sequence of events is. You can also ask the child to tell you his or her reactions to the text.

CALCULATING ERROR, ACCURACY, AND SELF-CORRECTION RATES

Your notations about the child's reading behavior become the data for determining teaching strategies and materials by using a few simple formulas. The *error rate* and *accuracy rate* indicate whether a book is at a child's easy/independent, instructional, or difficult/frustration reading level. Knowing a child's reading level will allow you to select appropriate books for instruction. A book that is at a child's easy/independent reading level is inappropriate for instruction because the text will not challenge the child; he or she will not be compelled to bring different reading strategies into play. Like-

---

Chart 7

Sample Reading Record: Errors and Self-Corrections

Text as Child Read It	Text with Teacher's Reading Record Notations	Reading Behavior(s)	Number of Errors	No. of Self-Corrections
Ben helps Anne make the bed.	Ben helps Anne ~~with~~ *make* the bed.	Substitution	1	0
Anne helps Dad make the garden.	Anne helps Dad ~~with~~ *make* the garden.	Substitution	1	0
Ben helps m-...Mom with the f-...paint...painting.	Ben helps Mom with the painting. *m— f-/paint/sic*	Using letter cues Self-correction	0	1
And along comes Jake!	And (then) along comes Jake!	Omission	1	0
Mom helps Dad make the car.	Mom helps Dad ~~with~~ *make* the car.	Substitution	1	0
Dad helps Ben with the washing.	Dad helps Ben with the washing.	Correct reading	0	0
Anne helps Mom with the b-...clean.	Anne helps Mom with the bathroom. *b-/clean*	Substitution	1	0
And along comes Jake!	And (then) along comes Jake!	Omission	1	0
Ben helps Dad with the windows.	Ben helps Dad with the windows.	Correct reading	0	0
Dad helps Mom with the wood.	Dad helps Mom with the wood.			
Mom helps Ben with the bike.	Mom helps Ben with the bike.			
		Total:	**6**	**1**

wise, a book at a child's difficult/frustration reading level is inappropriate because the child will not understand the meaning of the book—and therefore will not be able to utilize reading strategies when encountering difficult text. The *self-correction rate* provides a measure of how well a child is able to use reading strategies independently.

First, you need to count the errors that the child has made while reading. This information is necessary to determine the error and accuracy rates. Refer to the explanations below to determine whether or not a behavior is an error.

- **Substitution** is an error. Count each substitution as an error if the child substitutes the same word throughout the story (for example, if a child says "dog" every time the word *puppy* appears in the text). However, if a child substitutes a proper name for another proper name at the beginning of the story and continues to use that substitution throughout (for example, if the child says "Grumpy" or "Mr. Grouch" instead of "Mr. Grump"), count the substitution as an error only once. Because there is nothing in terms of meaning or syntax to cue the child to the error, we count that type of error only once.

- **Omission** is an error each time it occurs.

- **Insertion** is an error each time it occurs.

- **Using letter cues** is an error if the child cannot figure out the word. It is *not* an error if the child manages to decode the word.

- **Repetition** of correct text is not an error.

- **Self-correction** is not an error.

Chart 7, "Sample Reading Record: Errors and Self-Corrections," uses the analysis of the sample reading of *Along Comes Jake* as an example of how to determine which behaviors are errors and how to count the number of errors and self-corrections. (A filled-in reading record for this sample reading is shown on page 65 and a blank Reading Record reproducible is on page 81.)

Using the numbers generated by the reading, you can then calculate the error rate. The error rate is a ratio that compares the number of errors to the number of words read correctly.

Determine the error rate by following the steps outlined below.

First, count the total number of words in the text. (In cases where a child accidentally skips two pages because he or she turned two pages together, simply subtract the number of words on those pages.) There are sixty-four words in our sample text from *Along Comes Jake*. Write "64" in the blank that is next to "Words/Errors" on the Reading Record form.

Next, count the total number of errors. Then divide the total number of words by the total number of errors. The sample reading contains six errors, so "64/6" is written next to "Words/Errors" on the Reading Record form. Thus, the equation is $64/6 = 10.7$. The final number shows that the child made one error for every 10.7 words read. The error-rate ratio would be written this way:

1:10.7

Write this ratio after "Error Rate" on the form.

The error rate is then used to determine the accuracy rate. The accuracy rate indicates the percentage of text that the child is reading accurately. A quick way to determine the accuracy rate is to use chart 8, "Error/Accuracy Rates."

Chart 8

Error/Accuracy Rates

Error Rate	Accuracy Rate (%)	Reading Level
1: 200	99.5	Easy/independent reading level
1: 100	99	
1: 50	98	
1: 35	97	
1: 25	96	
1: 20	95	
1: 17	94	Instructional reading level
1: 14	93	
1: 12.5	92	
1: 11.75	91	
1: 10	90	
1: 9	89	Difficult/frustration reading level
1: 8	87.5	
1: 7	85.5	
1: 6	83	
1: 5	80	
1: 4	75	
1: 3	66	
1: 2	50	

Locate the error rate that you have calculated in the first column of the chart. Read across to find the corresponding percentage in the "Accuracy Rate" column. The last column in the chart translates the data in terms of the child's reading level. In our example, an error rate of 1:10.7 corresponds to an accuracy rate of 90 percent and a reading level that is borderline instructional for the child.

You can also calculate the accuracy rate using the formula below, in which E equals the total number of errors and W equals the total number of words in the text.

$$100 - \left(\frac{E}{W} \times 100 \right) = \text{percentage of text read correctly}$$

The equation looks like this when filled in with the numbers from the sample reading record:

$$100 - \left(\frac{6}{64} \times 100 \right) = 90.6$$

You would write "90.6%" after "Accuracy Rate" on the form.

Error and accuracy rates are calculated in order to determine the level at which a child is reading. Chart 8 shows how the error and accuracy rates correspond with reading levels. For example, the accuracy rate for the child reading *Along Comes Jake* is 90.6 percent, which means *Along Comes Jake* is right on the border between the frustration and the instructional reading levels. When a book is borderline in this way, you may wish to choose a new book that is clearly at the instructional level.

As mentioned earlier, a book at a child's frustration reading level is unsuitable for instruction because the child will be unable to gain a solid sense of the story and so will not be able to apply strategies when he or she meets difficulties. The reading will be frustrating, not challenging. A book at a child's easy/independent reading level is also a poor choice for instruction because the text does not challenge the child to use a variety of reading strategies. A book at the child's instructional level, however, provides the right balance between support and challenges that spur the use of reading strategies.

Once you have determined the error and accuracy rates, proceed to the calculation of the self-correction rate using the formula below, in which E is the number of errors and SC is the number of self-corrections:

$$\frac{(E + SC)}{SC} = X, \text{ where } X \text{ is the second half of the self-correction ratio of } 1:X.$$

Using the results of the child's reading of *Along Comes Jake*, the equation would look like this:

$$\frac{(6 + 1)}{1} = \frac{7}{1} = 7$$

Thus, the self-correction rate is 1:7, indicating that the child corrected 1 error for every 7 errors made.

Self-correction rates of 1:3 to 1:5 are considered good. But don't disregard even a poor self-correction rate. Any effort at self-correction can be guided so that children can become more aware of this strategy and learn to self-correct even more as they read, truly learning from their mistakes. Suggestions for how to guide children to self-correct are discussed in the "Strategies for Teaching" section below.

ANALYZING READING BY USING A READING RECORD

For your convenience, we have provided a Reading Record form that enables you to make all your notations and notes on one sheet of paper. A full-size, blank version of the form for photocopying is provided on page 81. Shown is a filled-in Reading Record for Eric's reading of *Along Comes Jake*. In this section, we discuss the use of a reading record step by step, with Eric's reading record as a reference.

First, fill in the child's name, the date, and the title and level of the book at the top of the form. The text from the book (or a portion thereof) is written or typed in the column labeled "Text," with one page of emergent level text on each line. This is the text on which you will write your notations as the child reads. For accessibility in taking a reading record on any material at any time, you may wish to use a blank form or piece of paper with no text written on it. You can simply make a check mark ($\sqrt{}$) for every correct word read.

As the child retells the story after reading it, fill in the appropriate spaces in the section labeled "Retelling." The headings "Complete/Almost complete," "Adequate," and "Limited" refer to how well the child understood and

Reading Record

Name: Eric

Title of Book: Along Comes Jake (pp 2-12)

Date: 10/28

Level of Book: 1

Independent Reading Level
- [ ] Easy (set F)
- [ ] Instructional
- [X] Difficult

E	SC	Text	M	S	V	Comments
I		*make* Ben helps Anne with the bed.	✓	✓		Used pictures to predict. Grammatically correct. M/W confusion?
I		*make* Anne helps Dad with the garden.	✓	✓		" " "
	I	*m— f-/paint/sc* Ben helps Mom with the painting.	✓		✓	Used initial consonant to predict. Cross-checked last word visually.
I		And (then) along comes Jake!			✓	Used 1-to-1 matching while reading but didn't monitor omission.
I		*make* Mom helps Dad with the car.	✓	✓		Used picture to predict. (M)- and (S)-based.
		Dad helps Ben with the washing.				Hesitated at "washing." Indicates use of cross-checking cues!
I		*b-/clean* Anne helps Mom with the bathroom.	✓			error meaning-based; sounded consonant; error not cross-checked with structure
I		And (then) along comes Jake!			✓	same omission as before
		Ben helps Dad with the windows.				} Correct reading
		Dad helps Mom with the wood.				
		Mom helps Ben with the bike.				
6	1	◄ Totals				

*M = meaning
S = structure
V = visual

Words: 64
Errors: 6

Error Rate: 1: 10.7   Accuracy Rate: 90.6%   Self-Correction Rate: 1:7

Retelling:	Complete/ Almost complete	Adequate	Limited
Characters	✓		
Events		✓	
Settings	✓		

Need to elicit more details? [ ] Many [X] Some [ ] None

General comments: Uses picture clues as meaning source. Substitutions all based within meaning structure. One self-correction. Used one-to-one but isn't monitoring omissions. Used some initial consonants.

Reading Proficiency:
- [ ] Fluent
- [X] Word by word
- [ ] With choppy phrasing

Teaching strategies: Develop awareness of 1-to-1 mismatch. Teach strategy of repeating at monitored error. Praise efforts to self-correct. Continue to reinforce use of sounding initial consonants to predict. Future focus: cross-checking cues.

about the child's reading strategies and use of the three reading cue systems, which will in turn enable you to guide that child effectively. Begin by refreshing your memory of the three reading cue systems if necessary: semantic (meaning), syntactic (grammar or structure), and graphophonic (sound and symbol, or visual).

The central column labeled "Cues Used" is divided into three columns labeled "M" (meaning), "S" (structure), and "V" (visual). Examine your notations and ask yourself questions about the child's responses in determining which cue system the child used (successfully or not) or neglected to use. It is easiest to ask yourself, "What strategy or cue system was the child using when the error occurred?" (Suggested questions to ask yourself are listed in chart 9, "Identifying Cue Systems," on page 66.) Check the appropriate box.

In the column labeled "Comments," write down your thoughts and any observations you made while listening to and watching the child read. These notes help to clarify the reasons behind your notations and your check marks.

For example, look at the place on Eric's Reading Record where he read the text "Ben helps Mom with the painting." The child first made an *f* sound, presumably getting ready to say "fence" (because he was responding to the illustration on this page, which features a fence). He quickly realized that the initial letter in this word was *p* and said "paint" instead, thus using a visual cue. He then self-corrected his reading and said "painting," using a structure cue. One generally helps somebody with *painting*, not with *paint*. *Painting* is the proper language structure for this sentence.

Next, analyze the child's reading behavior in its entirety. Step back and look at your

remembered the story's characters, events, settings, and other details. Check off the appropriate response to the query "Need to elicit more details?" as well. You may also briefly jot down what the child says during the retelling and later determine the elements that he or she has included.

Note how many running words are in the reading sample and how many errors were made next to "Words/Errors." Determine the error, accuracy, and self-correction rates using the marks you made in the first two columns labeled "E" (errors) and "SC" (self-corrections) based on your notations in the text. Record the results of your calculations where indicated on the Reading Record form. Check off the reading level in the upper right ("Easy," "Instructional," "Difficult").

Now you can analyze the child's reading behavior. Your analysis will yield information notations. Then ask yourself these questions: Which cues were used successfully, unsuccessfully, or not at all? Is the child self-correcting, and if so, what prompted him or her? Does the child use multiple strategies to overcome problems? Is he or she cross-checking by using another cue system?

Jot down your thoughts, observations, conclusions, and questions in the areas labeled "General comments" and "Teaching strategies." It's important to do so in deciding which teaching strategy will suit the child's needs, because without stepping back to take a "wide-screen view" of the child's efforts, you run the risk of homing in on one problem spot and losing the context of the child's overall reading ability.

Once you have considered the reading record as a whole, you are ready to decide upon and implement teaching strategies, which are discussed below. Remember, your teaching should reflect a balance of the reading cue systems, too. If a child relies too heavily on one system, it may be a sign that teaching strategies need to be examined.

IDENTIFYING APPROPRIATE TEACHING STRATEGIES

You've taken reading records of the children in your class. You've determined which reading strategies different children are able to use effectively and which strategies you may need to model and guide them to use. With every reading record, you will find that you are becoming increasingly attuned to the nuances of each child's reading ability. You will want to choose teaching strategies that make use of the information gathered in your evaluations and that guide children to become independent readers. The teaching strategies explained in the next section deal with developing concepts of print, guiding children to use the cue systems, focusing on specific types of errors, and bolstering independent reading skills through self-correction.

A handy checklist to use in keeping track of the entire class's progress in mastering concepts of print and various reading strategies is on page 76. This reproducible form is called the Concepts of Print Checklist (Emergent Levels): Class

---

Chart 9

Identifying Cue Systems

Type	General Questions	Specific Questions
1. Substitution	Was meaning retained? What strategy(ies) did the child use effectively?	Why do you think the child chose those particular words? Are they visually similar to the written words? Did they fit in grammatically?
2. Omission	Was meaning retained? What strategy(ies) did the child use effectively?	Why do you think the child changed the text? Was it grammatically correct with the omission?
3. Insertion	Was meaning retained? What strategy(ies) did the child use effectively?	What was the child doing when he/she inserted those words? Was the text grammatically correct with the insertions?
4. Letter Cues	Was meaning retained? What strategy(ies) did the child use effectively?	Is sounding out enough of a clue? Is the child able to use any other strategy to help? Were individual letters used/blended? Did the child use syllables, word families, or phrases?
5. Repetition	Was meaning retained? What strategy(ies) did the child use effectively?	What do you think might have caused the child to go back and repeat those parts? What word was next?
6. Self-Correction	Was meaning retained? What strategy(ies) did the child use effectively?	What caught the child's attention and caused him or her to have a change of mind?

Chart 10

Developing Concepts of Print

Directional Movement	• Have the child place a piece of gummed paper or a colored dot at the appropriate position on the page to indicate where one begins reading the text. • Use Big Books; the exaggerated eye movement necessary for reading the text locks in directional patterns. • Take the child's hand or finger and move it along the text as he or she helps you to read a story from a Big Book. • Model top-to-bottom directionality and return sweep with a Big Book text.
One-to-One Correspondence	• Hold and gently squeeze the child's hand as you move it along with your own, pointing to the words. • Have the child read aloud and point to the words with his or her finger while you point to the words with a pointer. • "Freeze" at the point where the child makes an error.
Words and Letters	• Print the words on separate cards. • Have the child match the words to the text. • Have the child frame words in the text with his or her fingers. • Have the child locate two words that are the same. • Have the child count the number of words on a sentence strip of story text. • Have the child locate one letter, two letters, a first letter, and a last letter. (Many children do not understand the difference between letters and words. The concepts of "first" and "last" are also frequently misunderstood.) Note whether the child repeatedly confuses certain letters (e.g., m/w, b/d).
Punctuation	• Point to a mark and ask, "What is this?" • Then ask, "Can you find another one?" • Ask, "What does it [the punctuation mark] mean?" Or, "What is it for?" • Ask, "How would you read the sentence?"

Profile. You'll find that many of the items in this checklist reflect the questions posed in the Concepts of Print Checklist (Emergent Levels): Individual Profile explained earlier. There is also a section in which to record information about reading strategies taken from your reading records.

This class profile is useful for analyzing a class as a whole and looking for patterns. Ask yourself these questions as you look over your checklist:

- Do some groups of children require similar guidance?

- Would some children work well in pairs?

- Could I model some things during Shared Reading that would benefit the whole class or groups of children?

- Are there specific books in which the use of print concepts would meet a group's or an individual child's needs?

Keep in mind, too, that you will want to share with parents or other caregivers specific strategies that they can help develop at home as their children read to them.

How Often Should You Take a Reading Record?

You'll probably find that it's useful to take a reading record for each child in your class at least once each month or each grading period and more often with children who need special attention. A child's reading records collected over a period of time provide a pattern of reading development. Simultaneously, you will develop your "reading-record ear." You'll encourage the use of reading strategies rather than merely "correct" word-by-word reading.

Strategies for Teaching

There are a variety of strategies for helping children develop various concepts of print. One strategy is to model the concepts during a

Chart 11

Guiding Reading Strategies

Cue System	Pointing Out Miscue	Modeling	Guiding	Reinforcing and Checking
Semantics (meaning)	"You said _____. Does that make sense?"	Read back the sentence and say, "Is that right? Skip the problem word and read the rest of the sentence and see if you can think of a word that might make sense."	"What do you think it might be?"	"Were you right? How did you figure it out?"
Syntax (grammatical structure)	"You said _____. Does that sound right?"	Reread the sentence with fluent phrasing and stop at the problem word.	"Read that again."	"Were you right? How did you figure it out?"
Graphophonic (sound/symbol, visual)	"Does that look right?"	Reread the sentence and just say the first sound of the problem word. Cover the word. Ask, "What would you expect to see at the beginning? After the letter ____?" Uncover the word and check.	"Does that look right?" "What would you expect to see if that word were ____?" "What letter does it start with? What sound does it make?" "Read the sentence again, saying the sound of the first letter, and see if you can think of what the word might be."	"Were you right? How did you figure it out?"
Cross-checking (checking one cue against another)	"It could be _____, but look at _____."	Insert possible words until the child can confirm the response using initial and final letters.	"Check to see if what you read looks and sounds right to you."	Show your confidence in the child's ability to figure it out.

Shared Reading and then focus on them specifically during a mini language lesson in a Guided Reading. Another is to pair children and have them read to each other. You might have children from a "buddy classroom," older children, or parent or other adult helpers read with your students. Specific guidelines for helping children to understand basic concepts of print are suggested in chart 10, "Developing Concepts of Print," on page 67.

Strategies for guiding children to use the cue systems are listed in chart 11, "Guiding Reading Strategies." The first column in chart 11 lists the three reading cue systems and cue cross-checking. For each cue system, four strategies for guiding children are listed:

1. Pointing out the miscue
2. Modeling how to read back a sentence and use the cue system to figure out the miscued word
3. Guiding the child to understand the process he or she is using
4. Reinforcing and checking the use of the cue system

These strategies can be used either in one-on-one sessions with individual children or in Guided Reading group sessions.

Sometimes, you will find that a child is not even aware that an error has been made. You'll need to alert the child and get him or her to realize that something is wrong by asking questions: "Did that sound right? Does that make sense?"

Modeling the use of a reading strategy is sometimes necessary, too. You can model for the child the process of rereading a sentence and using a different cue system to get over the hurdle of the difficult word. Once you have modeled a reading strategy, you may need only to ask a question that will guide the child to use it. And if the child is already using a reading strategy successfully, you'll simply need to reinforce the behavior. You might say

- Good work! You are really reading to see if the story makes sense. (meaning cues)

- Good work! You knew that _____ sounded right, didn't you? (structure cues)

- Good work! You are really paying attention to initial/final sounds. (visual cues)

You may also want to check the child's knowledge and increase the child's awareness of his or her own reading strategies. You might say, "Very good! How did you figure that out? How did you know what that word was?"

Finally, you will want to make sure that children can cross-check—that is, use a second reading strategy to validate the results of the first one. For example, you might engage in a discussion such as the following one, which is about page 6 in *The Long, Long Tail* (SUNSHINE Level 1, Set B):

T: Yes, the word *rug* makes sense. What letter would it start with if it were *rug*?
C: *R.*
T: What letter starts this word?
C: *M.*
T: Can you think of a word that means the same and starts with *m*?
C: *Mat.*
T: Slide your finger under the word and say it.
C: *(Sliding finger under the word.)* Mat.
T: How will you remember that this word is *mat*?
C: 'Cause it starts with an *m*.

Many teachers focus on specific concepts of print and on reading strategies during Guided Reading in addition to their continual formal and informal evaluation of children's development during the school day. You can use the Guided Reading Quick Evaluation Sheet during Guided Reading as a tool for measuring your students' understanding of print concepts and use of reading strategies. (A filled-out example is shown on page 58; a full-size version for photocopying is provided on page 77.) The sheet does not itemize skills; rather, it is designed to be filled out in accordance with the concepts and strategies you decide to emphasize with that group.

Learning to self-correct is one of the most important skills in a child's gaining independence in reading. Children need to know how to correct their own errors and alert themselves when text simply doesn't make sense or sound right. Guidelines for reinforcing children's efforts at self-correcting are listed in chart 12, "Building Self-Correction," on page 70. Examples of a child's reading behavior are given in the left-hand column. Explanations and approaches are detailed in the other four columns.

6

Chart 12

Building Self-Correction

Reading Behavior	Explanation of Behavior	Action to Take	What Teacher Might Say	Checking/Confirming Strategy
Child self-corrects.	The child is monitoring his or her own reading, searching for clues, cross-checking, and correcting own errors.	Praise.	"I liked the way you figured out what was wrong all by yourself! How did you figure that out so cleverly?"	Need to bring knowledge to a conscious level. Ask the child how he or she knew to make the correction.
Child unsuccessfully attempts to self-correct.	The child recognizes an error but either chooses an inappropriate strategy or fails to use an appropriate strategy effectively.	1. Determine which strategy the child attempted to use. 2. Reinforce the effort to self-correct. 3. Guide the child to use a different strategy or provide more guidance in using the strategy chosen.	"I liked the way you tried to figure that out. What word would make sense? Go back and read that again. What letter does it start with?"	Need to decide whether the child chose an appropriate strategy effectively before deciding how to guide.
Child reads through errors, then goes back to self-correct.	The child has been cued but lets it go and keeps reading.	Give the child time to catch the error. Let him or her read on. Don't do anything.	Nothing.	Doing nothing allows a child to self-correct naturally and on his or her own, building independence.
Child reads through errors and never self-corrects.	1. The child may have self-corrected the meaning internally but doesn't feel it is necessary to go back and correct the error orally. 2. The child doesn't realize an error has been made.	1. Ask the child to tell you about the story or even just that part. 2. Ask the child to go back and check the page on which the error was made.	"You misread something on this page. Can you find it? I like the way you did that, but can you find what part of this story was hard for you?"	Be sure to check to see if the child has a sense of the meaning of the part of the story that was read incorrectly.
Child pauses.	The child has noticed that something is not right, has lost the sense, or has met a challenge he or she cannot solve.	Draw attention to the fact that the child has become aware of something. Model a new strategy or guide the child to use a strategy he or she already knows.	"My, aren't you looking and checking! Why did you stop? What did you notice? You noticed something, didn't you? Aren't you clever!"	Support and encourage independence by drawing attention to and praising the child's awareness that something was wrong. Children need to learn to recognize and trust these signals.
Child stops and cannot continue.	The child cannot use any clues to solve a reading challenge.	Occasionally you may need to offer a choice of words. Have the child decide which one would fit best. Have the child confirm the word's appropriateness. The more you provide children with the one correct word, the further they will be from reading independently.	"How could you check?" "Would _____ make sense? Could _____ fit there? Do you think it looks like _____?"	This action will help develop a child's strategic thinking, draw attention to his or her abilities, and build independence.

A Review of Guided Reading Cue Systems and Strategies

Children use cues and strategies to help them unlock the concepts of print and the meaning of text. The ways in which a child uses the cues and strategies can tell the teacher a great deal about what that child knows about reading. These cues are

- **Meaning (semantics):** based on children's prior knowledge and their sense of story. Meaning cues also come from the text and illustrations.

- **Structure or grammar (syntax):** based on children's understanding of grammatical patterns, language structures, and knowl-

edge of English. Structure cues also come from the child's own natural language.

- **Visual or graphic (graphophonics):** based on children's knowledge of letter-sound relationships and print conventions. Visual cues also come from the child's understanding of letters and words.

Beginning emergent readers tend to rely heavily on one cue system, generally the visual/graphophonic. Good readers independently use the three cue systems within the reading process so quickly that their use may appear to be simultaneous.

The cue systems are shown in detail in chart 13, "The Three Reading Cue Systems." (This chart was first discussed in chapter 1, "Introduction to Guided Reading," and is repeated here with this more specific discussion.) The teacher's

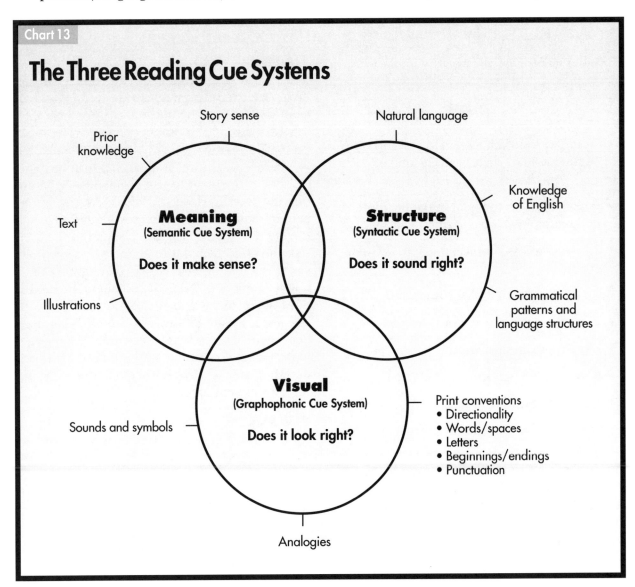

Chart 13

The Three Reading Cue Systems

Prior knowledge — Story sense — Natural language

Text — Illustrations

Meaning
(Semantic Cue System)

Does it make sense?

Structure
(Syntactic Cue System)

Does it sound right?

Knowledge of English

Grammatical patterns and language structures

Sounds and symbols

Visual
(Graphophonic Cue System)

Does it look right?

Print conventions
- Directionality
- Words/spaces
- Letters
- Beginnings/endings
- Punctuation

Analogies

6

objective in assisting students to read should be to encourage children to use the three cue systems appropriately and successfully so that the children will become independent readers.

Questions and Answers About Guided Reading

Q: *What can I say or do to guide a child to use a specific strategy?*

A: You can guide the child to use a specific strategy or cue system through focused questions:

MEANING

- You said _____. Did that make sense?
- Look at the pictures.
- What happened in the story when...?

STRUCTURE

- You said _____. Did that sound right?
- Can you reread that?

VISUAL

- Does that look right?
- What letter do you expect to see at the beginning/in the middle/at the end of _____?
- What sound do you hear at the beginning/in the middle/at the end of _____?
- Can you get your mouth ready to say that sound?
- Can you point to the words/letters?
- Can you match those words/letters?
- Were there enough words?
- Can you find that word/letter?
- Do you know a word like that?
- Do you know a word that starts/ends with those letters?

Q: *How do I correct a child who reads the wrong word?*

A: If a child reads a word incorrectly, first focus the child on the strategy that he or she was using when the error occurred.

MEANING CUES

Children seldom make meaning errors while reading. If a child uses meaning cues, generally an error is not made. When a child self-corrects an error, meaning is often the reason for the self-correction. Children want what is read to make sense to them. For example, the text said, "The baby is little and cute." The child read, "The baby is little and cut" and immediately self-corrected to "The baby is little and cute." The child was using visual/graphic cues when the error was made but used meaning to self-correct because what was read didn't make sense to the child. In this case, your comment might be, "You really did a good job of going back and rereading this part so that it would make sense," or "You're right, *cut* and *cute* do begin the same, but *cut* didn't make sense in this story." As an alternative, you could simply ask the child why he or she went back and self-corrected.

STRUCTURE CUES

If the child was using structure cues when the error occurred, you might want to focus on visual and/or meaning strategies. For example, the text said, "This is my puppy." The child read, "This is my dog." This type of misreading is common in natural language or structure.

Direct the child to use visual cues to figure out the word. Have the child say the letter/sound found in the incorrect word and then ask the child to locate that letter/sound in the text. Ask the child what letter/sound he or she does see in the text or what that word might be. You might comment, "Yes, *dog* sounds right and it does make sense in this story, but let's look at the word. Could that word be *dog?* What does *dog* begin with? What does this word begin with? What do you think it could be? Get your mouth ready to say the beginning sound and reread this sentence."

VISUAL CUES

If the child was using visual cues when the error occurred, you might want to focus on meaning or structure or both. For example, the text said, "Ben lives in a house." The student read, "Ben lives in a horse." It is common for a child to look only at the initial sound of a word and not pay attention to the rest of the word or to the meaning of the sentence.

Guide the child to use meaning to discover if the sentence/picture is about a horse. Ask, "What else would make sense here?" or "Where else could Ben live?" You might comment, "Yes, that could be *horse*. This word begins like *horse*, but would *horse* make sense in the story? What would make sense in this story?"

Q: *What if a child makes an error and then self-corrects?*
A: This is exactly what you want to happen! Self-correction is an important step toward reading independence and a self-improving system.

When children self-correct a word or words:

- They have noticed or heard something is wrong.

- They have taken a more careful look.

- They have applied a new strategy to get it right.

You can guide children to self-correct by asking carefully focused questions:

- There was a tricky part here. Can you find it?

- Can you reread that to see if it makes sense/sounds right/looks right?

- Were you right?

- Why did you stop/go back? What else did you notice?

- How did you know that was _____?

- It could be _____, but look at _____.

- It does look like it could be _____. Check to see if it makes sense/sounds right/looks right in this story.

The end goal of Guided Reading is to develop within each child a self-improving, self-extending system. The teacher's aim is to develop independent readers whose reading and writing improves each and every time they read and write.

According to Marie Clay, the independent student has strategies that are secure and habituated and that free the reader to attend to other concepts of reading. The independent reader

- Monitors his or her own reading and writing

- Searches for cues in meaning, in word sequences, in letter sequences

- Discovers new things for himself or herself

- Cross-checks one cue system against another

- Self-corrects, reflecting use of multiple strategies

- Strives to increase his or her speed, fluency, and accuracy

(Adapted from *Reading Recovery: A Guide for Teachers in Training* by Marie M. Clay [Heinemann 1993].)

The educator and author Yetta Goodman calls the observation of children "kidwatching." Just as a bird-watcher learns to identify birds that are far away by spotting the merest flicker of a wing or tail, so you will become an expert kidwatcher as you become attuned to catching the details in children's reading and writing behavior. The more you practice observing, evaluating, and tailoring teaching strategies to individual children's needs, the more fascinating this study will become.

6

Reproducibles

Concepts of Print Checklist (Emergent Levels): Individual Profile

Name: _____ Date: _____

Teacher Questions	+	✔	−	Concept
Before reading, ask the child:				
Where is the front of the book?				Book concepts—front cover
Where is the back of the book?				Book concepts—back cover
Can you point to the title?				Book concepts—title
Can you point to the title page?				Book concepts—title page
Which page do we read first?				Directionality—beginning of text
Where does it tell the story?				Reading concepts—print carries the message
Which way do we go when we're reading?				Directionality—left-to-right in a sentence
Where do we go when we get to the end of the line?				Directionality—return sweep
During reading, ask yourself:				
As the child reads and points to the text, is there an exact match between number of words spoken and number of words printed?				Reading concepts—one-to-one correspondence
After reading, ask the child:				
Can you put your fingers around a word?				Word concept
Can you find two words that are the same?				Word concept
Where is the first word on this page?				First word
Where is the last word on this page?				Last word
Can you put your fingers around a letter?				Letter concept
Can you tell me the names of some letters on the page?				Letter concept
Can you find a capital letter?				Capital letter
Can you find a small letter?				Small letter
What's this? . (period)				Punctuation marks
, (comma)				
? (question mark)				
" " (quotation marks)				

Notes:

Permission is given to teachers to reproduce this page for classroom use. © 1995 The Wright Group

Concepts of Print Checklist (Emergent Levels): Class Profile

Date: _____

Student Names

Directionality (demonstrates)
- Left-to-right page sequence
- Left-to-right in sentence
- Return sweep
- Reading top to bottom
- Starting at beginning of book
- Finishing at end of book

Reading Concepts (points to)
- Text (print tells the story)
- Each word (one-to-one correspondence)

Book Concepts (can identify)
- Cover of book
- Title
- Title page

Words/Letters (can identify)
- A letter
- A word
- The first word on a page
- The last word on a page
- A first letter
- A last letter
- A capital letter
- A small letter
- Names of some letters
- Key words in isolation

Punctuation (can identify)
- Question mark (?)
- Period (.)
- Comma (,)
- Quotation marks (" ")

Strategies Used
- Relies on memory for reading
- Uses pictures to tell story in own words
- Uses pictures to help with words
- Uses language patterns
- Uses structure knowledge
- Uses beginning letter sounds
- Uses many letter sounds
- Uses background experience

Permission is given to teachers to reproduce this page for classroom use. © 1995 The Wright Group

Guided Reading Quick Evaluation Sheet

Student Names

Skills

Notes

Permission is given to teachers to reproduce this page for classroom use. © 1995 The Wright Group

Concepts of Print Checklist (Early Fluency Level)

Date: _____

Names

Semantics (meaning)

Can identify:

Opposites

Compound words

Homophones

Synonyms

Vocabulary

Main idea

Words in languages other than English

Idioms

Syntax (grammar)

Can identify in books and use in writing:

Naming words (nouns)

Proper nouns

Action words (verbs)

Linking words (conjunctions)

Describing words (adjectives and adverbs)

Prepositions (location words)

Plurals

Pronouns

Word endings and their purposes

Simple sentences

Paragraphs

Graphophonics (sounds and symbols)

Can identify in books and use in writing:

Initial and final consonants and their sounds

Letter combinations and their sounds

Short vowel sounds

Long vowel sounds

Word families and their sounds

Rhyming words

Permission is given to teachers to reproduce this page for classroom use. © 1995 The Wright Group

Concepts of Print Checklist (Early Fluency Level) continued

Date: _____

Names

Punctuation

Can identify and give purpose of:

Period (.)															
Question mark (?)															
Exclamation point (!)															
Quotation marks (" ")															
Comma (,)															
Apostrophe (')															
Ellipses (...)															
Dash (—)															
Unusual typeface (bold, italic, etc.)															

Language Strategies

Uses semantic cue system:

Story sense															
Logic															
Background experience															
Pictorial and graphic resources															

Uses syntactic cue system:

Structure knowledge															
Language patterns															
Word endings															

Uses graphophonic cue system:

Beginning sounds															
Ending sounds															
Medial sounds															
Letter combinations															
Short and long vowel sounds															
Rhyming sounds															

Cross-checks (makes predictions using more than one cue system)

Permission is given to teachers to reproduce this page for classroom use. © 1995 The Wright Group

Concepts of Literature Checklist (Early Fluency Level)

Date: _____

Names

Story Structure (can identify)
Beginning, middle, and end
Characterization
Story climax
Sequence of events

Literary Terms (can identify)
Character
Hero/villain
Setting
Problem
Solution
Point of view
Dialogue
Author/illustrator
Stage directions
Genre: Fiction
    Nonfiction
    Diary/journal
    Biography
    Drama/play
    Poetry

Literary Devices (can identify)
Similes
Metaphors
Alliteration
Onomatopoeia
Exaggeration
Word play

Literary Strategies
Uses table of contents
Skims for facts
Uses dictionary/encyclopedia
Summarizes
Retells
Compares and contrasts
Questions

Permission is given to teachers to reproduce this page for classroom use. © 1995 The Wright Group

Reading Record

Name: _____

Title of Book: _____

Date: _____

Level of Book: _____

Independent Reading Level
☐ Easy
☐ Instructional
☐ Difficult

E	SC	Text	Cues Used*			Comments
			M	S	V	
	◄ Totals		*M = meaning S = structure V = visual			

Words / Errors : _____   Error Rate: _____   Accuracy Rate: _____   Self-Correction Rate: _____

Retelling:	Complete/ Almost complete	Adequate	Limited
Characters			
Events			
Settings			

Need to elicit more details? ☐ Many ☐ Some ☐ None

Reading Proficiency:
☐ Fluent
☐ Word by word
☐ With choppy phrasing

General comments:

Teaching strategies:

Permission is given to teachers to reproduce this page for classroom use. © 1995 The Wright Group

Also available: *Guided Reading at the Emergent Level* video (2 tapes)

To order this video, to receive a current catalog, or to get information on teacher training, contact

The Wright Group
19201 120th Avenue NE
Bothell, WA 98011-9512

or call toll free 1-800-523-2371